IDIOMS IN ACTION

A key to fluency in English

WITH   **10 COMMON IDIOM ERRORS (101)**
                 A STUDENT'S LOG OF IDIOMATIC ENGLISH (102)

George Reeves
Cuyahoga Community College

NEWBURY HOUSE PUBLISHERS, Cambridge
A division of Harper & Row, Publishers, Inc.
New York, Philadelphia, San Francisco, Washington
London, Mexico City, São Paulo, Singapore, Sydney

NEWBURY HOUSE PUBLISHERS
A division of Harper & Row, Publishers, Inc.

 Language Science
Language Teaching
Language Learning

CAMBRIDGE, MASSACHUSETTS

ISBN: 912066-63-6

Designed by Judith Lerner
Cover by Harry Swanson

Printed in the U.S.A.
63-24784

First printing: February 1975
Sixth printing: May 1978

21

Preface

This is a book born of embarrassment, boredom and skepticism.

EMBARRASSMENT: As a young American teacher of English at the Ecole Polytechnique of Paris, France, I was constantly asked by students "What does this word mean?" To them I was a walking dictionary. Sometimes, however, my definition didn't satisfy them and they tried to improve on it. I became embarrassed. One day I fought back.

"Now use the word in a sentence," I demanded.

They could not.

"Then what good is it being able to define words you can't use?" I said triumphantly. For in my embarrassment I had rediscovered that words must be contextualized to have meaning and to become a living part of one's knowledge.

BOREDOM: The boredom was that of my English-second-language students at Cuyahoga Community College, where I now teach. Language learning bored them—particularly idiom lists, definitions and drills. Yet idioms made up an important part of our program, and we needed material to encourage students to learn to speak and write idiomatic English.

SKEPTICISM: My wife is French, therefore skeptical. Glancing through an idiom book being used in my class, she asked: "Why don't you teach frequent idioms?"

"Can't you read?" I snapped. "The author says his idioms are frequent."

"I've never heard them."

If after four years in the United States she hadn't heard them, well, my students probably hadn't either. So why teach them idioms they would seldom hear? Or use?

They agreed with her. They had rarely heard native speakers using these idioms. Not only was I boring them; worse, I was teaching them a lot of useless English.

But how could I make everyday idioms amusing? To find an answer, I began creating contexts and experimenting with dialogues. In so doing, I got a great deal of advice and good-natured criticism from my colleagues who tried out these exercises in their classes. I especially wish to thank Phyllis Melnick and Ray Ackley for their insightful suggestions and Rose Gaynor for her excellent typing.

George Reeves
Cleveland, Ohio
January, 1975

To the Teacher of English

THE GOAL

Getting your students to understand, speak and write everyday idioms in everyday English.

THE APPROACH

Idioms in Action deals with 150 of the most frequent idioms in English. It provides practice in speaking and writing these idioms—practice which is repeated, extensive and carefully planned.

THE LEVEL OF USE

When are students ready to write English? We teachers don't agree. The first half of this book assumes only that they can recognize approximately 2,000 words,* understand the syntax of plain conversation and manipulate the simple past, the simple and progressive (continuous) present, and the simple future tense. Therefore, either advanced beginners or intermediate students can use this book, depending on the language curriculum and the teacher's decision.

THE RATIONALE

Why is it that students can memorize lists of idioms, parrot definitions, but fail to speak and write idiomatic English? A major reason seems to be lack of experience with idioms in contexts.

To be mastered, idioms must be used over and over in context. By experiencing and using them in related social and linguistic contexts, students learn them much more efficiently than by rote memory.** And although definitions and synonyms are helpful, something more is needed. Like the idioms they define, these words also need to be embedded in appropriate contexts—contexts which cue, correct and reinforce understanding, contexts which inform, amuse and relate to students' interests.

---

*Accounting for 95 percent of the words in exercises one to fifteen (based on *The New Horizon Ladder Dictionary of the English Language* by John Robert Shaw with Janet Shaw).

**See Kenneth L. Pike, *The Modern Language Journal*, 44.293-294 (November, 1960). Dr. Pike discusses language as a "structural part of a larger whole—part of life's total behavioral action and structure, intimately linked to social interaction." Commenting on the value of context in language exercises, he continues: "In the sentence *The big boy came home* there is a slot where the boy may be replaced by girl, man, etc. New vocabulary is learned most easily not through rote memory alone, but through the hearing or speaking of new words in such grammatical positions. The 'substitution' tables of British scholars or the 'pattern practice' of the English Language Institute, University of Michigan, etc., take advantage of this fact. Here the successfulness of such drills is not exclusively the result of sheer repetition, but to a very significant degree due to the psychological ties between the substituted words and their contexts."

SPECIFIC METHODS

1 Each part of an exercise emphasizes a particular problem; every part requires that the idiom agree in tense and person with its sentence. For example, Part A, although requiring such agreement, emphasizes spelling in that the student must write each idiom letter separately.

Example: Yesterday Anne *d i d* *h e s* *b e s t* to win.

Part B, by requiring the student to substitute the idiom for its bold-face equivalent, cues, channels and corrects his understanding.

Example: Mimi **tries really hard** to pass the test. *Mimi does her best to pass the test* .

Parts C and D require the student to use the idiom in context. Part C, with its five blanks for five idioms, asks for a simple contextual choice. Part D, with its six blanks for ten idioms (five of which "carry over" from the preceding exercise), demands a more difficult contextual choice.

Example: We wanted to swim well, so we *did our best* to practice every day.

Part E, by asking the student to substitute an idiom for its bold-face equivalent (as in B above) but to use his own words to complete the sentence, prepares him for the free idiomatic writing of Part F.

Example: I **tried really hard** to learn English when . . . .

I did my best to learn English when I visited New York.

Part F requires the student to write a paragraph using the five idioms on a familiar subject.

2 Testing: Ten tests help the student review the spelling, meaning and use of the idioms.

3 Memory aids: The idioms reappear in subsequent dialogues and exercises.

4 Use of spoken American English: The syntax, contractions and rhythms of spoken American English are used throughout in order that the student can form his prose on everyday language.

SUGGESTIONS TO THE TEACHER FOR CLASS USE

1 Ask your students to complete the *Sample Exercise.* If you explain the exercise to them and correct their mistakes in class, they will make fewer "careless" mistakes. Then, if they complete the *Student Checklist*, the number of such mistakes will go even lower.

2 Read aloud the dialogue between Mimi and Sam. Then read it again. However, this time ask your students to repeat each sentence after you.

3 Now your students are ready to complete the exercises. When they have completed them, read Parts A, B, C, and D with them so that they may correct their own mistakes.

4 After your students have completed Parts E and F, you may ask some of them to write Parts E and F on the blackboard. This will allow you to make corrections in grammar. It will also give each person in class an opportunity to say something about the exercises and to compare his or her answers. Encourage class discussion. (Weak students should omit Part F.)

5 You may collect the exercises from each student. You can correct them and return them to the student. After you collect the exercises, you may want your students to speak the idioms. You can do this by first reading the dialogue aloud. Stop reading when you come to the place where an idiom is to be put in. Ask your students to say which idiom belongs there. You may also ask a student to repeat the entire sentence from memory. Then read another sentence in the same way.

6 Use the same procedure as above (in paragraph 5) on the "question" parts (the fill-ins, sentence completions, etc.) and ask your students to speak their answers after they have written them.

7 After every third exercise, there is a three part *Test*. Out of 100 points, Part A counts 15 points. Part B counts 25 points. Part C counts 60 points. Ask your students to write Parts A and B as homework. These parts also serve to prepare them for their in-class oral (or written) test on Part C.

8 One student "plays" Sam. Another student "plays" Mimi. They act out the dialogue in front of the class. (Simple props—a chair or table—can make the situation more realistic.)

9 Have your students write an imitation of a dialogue—their own idiomatic commentary on American life—and take turns acting it.

10 The *Idiom Review Game*: After your class finishes a few exercises, divide it into opposing sides. Call alternatively on each side: A player must supply an appropriate sentence for the idiom given. If he cannot, he must stop playing. The side with the most players at the end wins the game.

11 Diagnostic notes for teachers on *10 Common Idiom Errors*—See page 101.

12 On page 102 *A Student's Log of Idiomatic English* helps students to note and define their problems in using idiomatic English.

Contents

To the Student of English

WHAT IS AN IDIOM?

An idiom says something in a special way. It is a group of words which can't be clearly understood from the ordinary meanings of its words. *In time* is an idiom. So is *on time*.

WHY STUDY IDIOMS THAT YOU ALREADY KNOW?

Because you don't really know them. You only recognize them. For example, you probably recognize *in time* and *on time*. But can you use them correctly in sentences?

No? Then it's like having a car in the garage but not knowing how to drive it.

In short, useless knowledge cannot help you. That is why *Idioms in Action* makes you *use, use, use* your everyday idioms. So do its exercises carefully. Soon you will—

1 Speak and write dozens of the most frequent (and useful!) idioms in the English language;
2 Sound less like a book and more like a human being;
3 Use your English better and better.

Part 1

PAST, PRESENT AND FUTURE TENSES (SIMPLE AND PROGRESSIVE)

Sample
Idiom Exercise

SAM: Be sure to complete this page!

MIMI: And complete the next three pages, too.

1. **ahead of time**
2. **at first**
3. **do** (my, your, her, his, our, their, etc.) **best**
4. **get mixed up**
5. **of course**

These are the five idioms which you will use in this sample exercise.

MIMI: English confuses me. I don't* understand it.

SAM: **I get mixed up,** too.

MIMI: **Mixed up**? I mix up flour and eggs to make a cake. You don't look like an egg to me.

SAM: **Of course,** I don't. It's not flour and eggs; it's my ideas that are mixed up.

MIMI: **To get mixed up** is an idiom, isn't it?

SAM: Right! You knew what its words meant separately, but you didn't know what they meant joined together. That's why idioms are difficult **at first.** Later they'll become easy.

MIMI: If I study them, they'll become easy. Isn't that what you mean?

SAM: If you **do your best,** you'll succeed.

MIMI: And I'll have grey hairs **ahead of time.**

This is the dialog which shows how th[e] five idioms ar[e] used.

COMPLETE ALL OF THE EXERCISES BELOW (Parts A,B,C,D,E, and F)

PART A   USING ALL FIVE IDIOMS, FILL IN THE BLANKS, ONE LETTER FOR EACH BLANK. MAKE EACH IDIOM AGREE IN TENSE AND PERSON WITH ITS SENTENCE.

EXAMPLE: Yesterday Anne _d i d_ _h e r_ _b e s t_ to win. *(Idiom 3)*
[person] — [tense]

Maria and Helena study hard. They |_|_|_| |_|_|_|_| |_|_|_|_| to learn English. *(Idiom [3])* That's why they like to finish their reading early and prepare their lessons |_|_|_|_|_| |_|_| |_|_|_|_|. |_|_| |_|_|_|_|_|_|, they are doing well in English. *(Idioms 1,5)*

But sometimes Maria and Helena become nervous during a test and |_|_|_| |_|_|_|_|_| |_|_| They write all the wrong answers |_|_| |_|_|_|_|_|. Afterwards they correct their mistakes. *(Idioms 4,2)*

*Contractions are on page 90. (A contraction is a shortened form. *Don't* is a contraction of *do not*.)

MY NAME _____ TEACHER'S NAME _____ DATE _____

PART B SOME WORDS BELOW ARE BOLD FACE.* SUBSTITUTE THE ABOVE IDIOMS WHICH MEAN THE SAME THING. THEN COPY THE COMPLETE SENTENCE IN THE SAME TENSE TENSE AND PERSON.

EXAMPLE: [tense and person] Mimi **tries really hard** to pass the test. *Mimi does her best to pass the test.*

1 Bill **tries really hard** to please his wife. _____ (Idiom 3)

2 **In the beginning**, I didn't understand math. _____ (Idiom 2)

3 My English class began ten minutes **early** today. _____ (Idiom 1)

_____

4 **Naturally**, I like to eat ice cream. _____ (Idiom 5)

5 Sam **becomes confused** when he doesn't read directions. _____ (Idiom 4)

_____

PART C WRITE THE APPROPRIATE IDIOM. MAKE IT AGREE IN TENSE AND PERSON WITH THE REST OF THE SENTENCE.

EXAMPLE: [tense] Sam didn't read directions and *got mixed up* .

Unlike Maria and Helena, John didn't study hard. He didn't _____ to learn English. He even hated to finish his homework early, so he never prepared his lessons _____ .

_____ , he was failing English. *(Idioms 3,1,5)*

In class John seldom knew the answers to his teacher's questions. He almost always _____ .

She accepted his excuses _____ , but now she no longer believes him. *(Idioms 4,2)*

PART D FILL IN THE BLANKS, USING ALL FIVE IDIOMS.

EXAMPLE: [person] We wanted to swim well, so we *did our best* to practice every day. [tense]

I wanted to arrive at the movies _____ or, at the latest, for the start of the film. But my boyfriend _____ in his directions and we took the wrong road.

Later, he admitted it was his own fault, but _____ he blamed me. I _____ to remain calm. _____ , we arrived late. *(Idioms 1,4,2,3,5)*

PART E SUBSTITUTE THE CORRECT IDIOMS FOR THE BOLD FACE WORDS. THEN COPY THE SENTENCE AND FINISH IT IN YOUR OWN WORDS. ANSWERS TO SENTENCE 1 COULD BE:

EXAMPLES: *I did my best to learn English when I visited New York.*
I did my best to learn English when I was at an American school.

Bold face means heavy type like **this** or like **this**. Throughout this book, the idioms and the words which define them will appear in bold face.

1 **I tried really hard** to learn English when . . . . _____

_____ *(Idiom 3)*

2 **Naturally,** American children like to . . . . _____

_____ *(Idiom 5)*

3 John **became confused** on his test because . . . . _____

_____ *(Idiom 4)*

4 If you finish your work **early**, you can . . . . _____

_____ *(Idiom 1)*

5 **In the beginning,** did he believe . . . ? _____

_____ *(Idiom 2)*

PART F   WRITE A PARAGRAPH ABOUT THE DAY YOU CAME TO CLASS WITHOUT YOUR BOOKS (OR PEN, OR HOMEWORK). USE ALL FIVE IDIOMS AND PUT A LINE UNDER THEM.

ANSWERS TO THE SAMPLE EXERCISE

PART A: . . . do their best . . . ahead of time . . . of course . . . get mixed up . . . at first

PART B: 1 Bill does his best to please his wife.
2 At first, I didn't understand math.
3 My English class began ten minutes ahead of time today.
4 Of course, I like to eat ice cream.
5 Sam gets mixed up when he doesn't read directions.

PART C: . . . do his best . . . ahead of time . . . of course . . . got mixed up . . . at first

PART D: . . . ahead of time . . . got mixed up . . . at first . . . did my best . . . of course

PART E: 1 I did my best to learn English when I visited New York.
I did my best to learn English when I was at an American school.
I did my best to learn English when I was a student in the U. S.
I did my best to learn English when I had an American girlfriend.
I did my best to learn English when I liked my teacher.   Etc.
2 Of course, American children like to play baseball.
Of course, American children like to read funny stories.
Of course, American children like to eat ice cream.
Of course, American children like to go to the movies.   Etc.
3 John got mixed up on his test because he didn't study enough.
John got mixed up on his test because he didn't read the directions.
John got mixed up on his test because he didn't remain calm.
John got mixed up on his test because he didn't follow his teacher's advice.   Etc.
4 If you finish your work ahead of time, you can watch TV.
If you finish your work ahead of time, you can listen to jazz.
If you finish your work ahead of time, you can go to a play.
If you finish your work ahead of time, you can help me with mine.   Etc.
5 At first, did he believe that John was right?
At first, did he believe Mary?
At first, did he believe what you told him?
At first, did he believe that we were friends?   Etc.

PART F: [1]I do my best to be in class ahead of time, but yesterday I got mixed up because my watch stopped and, of course, I was late for class.[2] I even forgot my books. At first,[3] my teacher was angry, but he smiled after I told him what happened.[4]

[1]When you begin to write a paragraph, leave an inch or an inch and a half of white space before you begin your first sentence. This is called "indenting." (One inch = about three centimeters.)

[2]Leave enough space between sentences to let your reader know that you are beginning a new sentence. A period (.) clearly made at the end of each sentence also helps. Capital letters (A,B,C,D,E, etc.) at the beginning of sentences help, too.

[3]Put a line under all five idioms.

[4]Every sentence *except the last one* must be written all the way to the right margin unless it stops before it reaches there. If it stops, you must begin a new sentence. You cannot leave unused space in the middle of your paragraph.

[5]Keep the margins of your paragraph even.

Student Checklist

EXERCISE 1 2 3 4 5 6 7 8 9 10 11 12 13 14 15 16 17 18 19 20 21 22 23 24 25 26 27 28 29 30

DIALOGUE   DID YOU?
read the dialogue carefully
memorize the spelling of the idioms
try to guess their meaning from the situation

PART A   DID YOU?
repeat the idioms aloud, and make a connection
between the pronunciation and the spelling.

PART B   DID YOU?
copy and punctuate correctly the complete sentence
check pronouns and tenses

PART C   DID YOU?
check the pronouns and tenses of the idioms

PART D   DID YOU?
check that each idiom is appropriate to its sentence
check pronouns and tenses

PART E   DID YOU?
check pronouns and tenses
complete the sentences in your own words
copy and punctuate correctly

PART F   DID YOU?
use related sentences (a paragraph)
include all five idioms

exercise 1

In the Language Lab:
Sam Meets Mimi

from now on
little by little
take care of
that's all
What's the matter?

SAM: **What's the matter**, Miss? You look unhappy.
MIMI: It's my tape recorder. **Little by little** the sound becomes weaker.
SAM: Perhaps I can **take care of** it. I work for the company which makes them. It's Japanese like I am.
MIMI: Why are you in America?
SAM: I'm here to study engineering and improve my English. And you?
MIMI: I want to become a translator. But please—why doesn't my machine work?
SAM: A wire is loose, **that's all**.
MIMI: Excuse me. Don't you sit behind me in English class?
SAM: Yes. May I introduce myself? I'm Hideki Samuhama, but my friends call me Sam.
MIMI: I'm Anne-Marie Bouvier. Please call me Mimi **from now on**. And thanks for your help, Sam.

PART A   USING ALL FIVE IDIOMS, FILL IN THE BLANKS, ONE LETTER FOR EACH BLANK. MAKE EACH IDIOM AGREE IN TENSE AND PERSON WITH ITS SENTENCE.

Jeff looks sad. His friends ask him, "⎿_⎽_⎽_⎽_⎽_⎽⏌' ⎿_⎽_⎽_⎽_⎽_⎽_⎽_⎽_⎽_⎽_⎽⏌?" He

answers, "I need a few dollars, ⎿_⎽_⎽_⎽_⎽⏌' ⎿_⎽_⎽_⎽⏌." Of course, Jeff's friends ⎿_⎽_⎽_⎽_⎽⏌

⎿_⎽_⎽_⎽_⎽_⎽⏌ ⎿_⎽⏌ his problem. They give him the money. ⎿_⎽_⎽_⎽_⎽_⎽_⎽_⎽_⎽_⎽⏌

⎿_⎽_⎽_⎽_⎽_⎽⏌ he becomes happier. ⎿_⎽_⎽_⎽_⎽_⎽_⎽_⎽_⎽⏌ Jeff knows that he has good

friends.

PART B   SOME WORDS BELOW ARE BOLD FACE. SUBSTITUTE THE ABOVE IDIOMS WHICH MEAN THE SAME THING. THEN COPY THE COMPLETE SENTENCE IN THE SAME TENSE AND PERSON.

1 We **gave attention to** our homework before class._____

2 **Gradually** the two men became friends. _____

3 **What's wrong?** You look unhappy. _____

4 (I failed my test today.) **From the present into the future** I'm going to study harder. _____

_____

5 Olga wants a glass of water, **nothing more.** _____

MY NAME _____ TEACHER'S NAME _____ DATE _____

PART C   FILL IN THE BLANKS. USE ALL FIVE IDIOMS IN THE CORRECT TENSE AND PERSON.

Olga seems nervous. An American asks her, " _____ ? " She replies, "I can't find my bus ticket, _____ ." The American _____ Olga's difficulty. He gives her a bus ticket. She slowly becomes less nervous. _____ she begins to relax. _____ Olga knows she'll feel comfortable in America.

PART D   FILL IN THE BLANKS, USING ALL FIVE IDIOMS PLUS ONE FROM THE SAMPLE EXERCISE.

Tuesday I didn't feel well. " _____ ? " my boss asked me. I said I felt sick. "Go home and _____ yourself," he told me. "You need a day's rest, _____ . Starting now, you must work less. _____ you must relax more."

Of course, I did what my boss told me. Wednesday I stayed home. Slowly, _____ _____ , I began to feel better. Thursday I went to work early. I arrived _____ _____ .

PART E   SUBSTITUTE THE CORRECT IDIOMS FOR THE BOLD FACE WORDS. THEN COPY THE WHOLE SENTENCE AND FINISH IT IN YOUR OWN WORDS.

1 **What was wrong?** Were you . . . ? _____

2 We lighted a fire and **gradually**. . . . _____

3 My wife **gave attention to** her housework before . . . . _____
_____

4 I only want . . ., **nothing more.** _____

5 **From the present into the future** I'm going to. . . . _____
_____

PART F   WRITE ONE PARAGRAPH ABOUT MEETING A STRANGER AND BECOMING HIS (HER) FRIEND. USE ALL FIVE IDIOMS.

COLORFUL IDIOM: **PAY THROUGH THE NOSE.** Pay too much for something.

exercise 2

Mimi and Sam Discuss France and Japan

as much as
change (one's) mind
come from
get rid of
go on

SAM: May I sit beside you? We have a few minutes before class begins.
MIMI: Oh, hello Sam. Certainly.
SAM: I see you're reading a French magazine.
MIMI: Yes, it's *L'Express*. I like to know what **is going on** in my country.
SAM: Where do you **come from** in France?
MIMI: From the loveliest city in the world–Paris.
SAM: You ought to visit Kyoto. You might **change your mind**. It has beautiful temples and its fifty-nine foot statue of Buddha is famous. But **as much as** I like Kyoto, I know there are other beautiful cities.
MIMI: You're right. I must **get rid of** the silly idea that Paris is the only beautiful city.
SAM: Anyway, lots of people feel the same as you do. Everybody loves Paris.

PART A   USING ALL FIVE IDIOMS, FILL IN THE BLANKS, ONE LETTER FOR EACH BLANK. MAKE EACH IDIOM AGREE IN TENSE AND PERSON WITH ITS SENTENCE.

Gloria likes American movies. But /_/_/_/_/_/_/_/_/ she likes them, she likes her English lessons better. Of course, she /_/_/_/_/_/_/_/_/_/_/_/_/_/_/ sometimes: She decides not to do her lessons but to go to the movies instead. A good film helps her to /_/_/_/_/_/_/ /_/_/ her sadness.

Why is Gloria sad? Because she /_/_/_/_/_/_/_/_/_/ Argentina but doesn't live there any more. It's difficult for her to learn what /_/_/_/_/_/_/_/_/_/ now in her native country.

PART B   SOME WORDS BELOW ARE BOLD FACE. SUBSTITUTE THE **ABOVE** IDIOMS WHICH MEAN THE SAME THING. THEN COPY THE COMPLETE SENTENCE IN THE SAME TENSE AND PERSON.

1 I **was a native of** Greece. _____

2 He **discards** his broken furniture immediately. _____

3 What's **happening**? Why is everyone shouting? _____

4 **Although** I like your cake, I can't eat another piece. _____
_____

5 I'm not going to France now; I **decided differently**. _____
_____

PART C WRITE THE APPROPRIATE IDIOM. MAKE IT AGREE IN TENSE AND PERSON WITH THE REST OF THE SENTENCE.

SALLY: Fred always seems to know what's _____ in England. Is that the country

he _____ ? Is he English?

JANE: Yes, he is.

SALLY: Do you know if he's rich?

JANE: I'm not sure. He owns a big, expensive English car. Of course, he likes it, but _____

he likes it, he says it uses too much gas. Perhaps he'll _____ about

keeping it. He can _____ it and buy a small, cheap car instead.

PART D FILL IN THE BLANKS, USING ALL FIVE IDIOMS PLUS ONE FROM EXERCISE 1.

My wife's family were natives of Miami, Florida. She _____ there, too. But

_____ I loved my wife, I wasn't able to like her family. Why? Because I never

knew ahead of time what they were thinking. I never knew what was _____ in their

minds. They had different opinions every day; they were always _____ . They

_____ their old opinions as easily as they discarded old furniture. _____

I'm going to do the same thing.

PART E SUBSTITUTE THE CORRECT IDIOMS FOR THE BOLD FACE WORDS. THEN COPY THE WHOLE SENTENCE AND FINISH IT IN YOUR OWN WORDS.

1 Many interesting things **happened** in Washington when. . . . _____

_____

2 Peter **is a native of**. . . . _____

3 If you need more space in your room, you must try to **discard**. . . ._____

_____

4 Unless I write my girlfriend, she is going to **decide differently** about. . . . _____

_____

5 **Although** Mary hated homework, she did . . . . _____

_____

PART F WRITE ONE PARAGRAPH ABOUT WHY YOU LOVE YOUR COUNTRY. USE ALL FIVE IDIOMS.

COLORFUL IDIOM: **PUT THE CART BEFORE THE HORSE.** Do things backward; say or arrange things in reverse order.

exercise 3
Mimi Invites Sam to Dinner

at home
get off
get on
have to
run into

MIMI: Sam! What a surprise to **run into** you at the supermarket! I thought you always ate in restaurants.
SAM: Restaurants cost too much. I eat **at home**.
MIMI: So do I. I **have to** cook all my own meals.
SAM: I'm very good at opening cans. The less cooking I do, the happier I am.
MIMI: **Why don't you come** to dinner at my apartment Saturday night? I'll cook for you.
SAM: At your apartment?
MIMI: Don't look surprised. It's what girls do here. In America it isn't considered wrong.
SAM: Well, I'm happy to accept your invitation. Please tell me where you live.
MIMI: At 5 Maple Avenue. Be sure to **get on** the Baker Hill bus. **Get off** at 33rd Street. Maple is the street with the bank on the corner. You can't miss it.

PART A   USING ALL FIVE IDIOMS, FILL IN THE BLANKS, ONE LETTER FOR EACH BLANK. MAKE EACH IDIOM AGREE IN TENSE AND PERSON WITH ITS SENTENCE.

Mimi's neighbors usually stay /_/_/ /_/_/_/_/ and play loud music until midnight. On weekends the noise doesn't bother her, because she can sleep late. But on weekdays she /_/_/_/_/_/_/ wake up at seven and make breakfast. At 7:45 she /_/_/_/_/_/_/_/ a bus and rides to work. She often /_/_/_/_/_/_/_/_/_/ her noisy neighbors on the bus; she doesn't say hello even though they /_/_/_/_/_/_/_/ at the same stop as she does.

PART B   SOME WORDS BELOW ARE BOLD FACE. SUBSTITUTE THE ABOVE IDIOMS WHICH MEAN THE SAME THING. THEN COPY THE COMPLETE SENTENCE IN THE SAME TENSE AND PERSON.

1 Mimi **entered** the plane at Chicago. _____

2 I often **accidentally meet** friends on the street. _____

_____

3 I prefer staying **in my house** on rainy evenings. _____

_____

MY NAME _____ TEACHER'S NAME _____ DATE _____

4 Helen **must** work to pay for her food and clothing. _____

_____

5 Sam **left** the boat at San Francisco. _____

PART C   WRITE THE APPROPRIATE IDIOM. MAKE IT AGREE IN TENSE AND PERSON WITH THE REST OF THE SENTENCE.

Eve seldom stayed _____. She travelled a lot and, of course, she drove her car everywhere. But when she lost her job, she _____ sell it and travel by train instead.

Yesterday Eve wanted to go downtown, but when she _____ the train, she _____ her old boss. This meeting made her so unhappy that she _____ at the next stop and returned home.

PART D   FILL IN THE BLANKS, USING ALL FIVE IDIOMS PLUS ONE FROM EXERCISE 2.

When I _____ old friends, I'm always happy to see them. But when I _____ the subway yesterday and sat down beside George, I didn't recognize him at first. His hair was long and he was wearing dark glasses.

He told me that his wife _____ about their marriage and that she was divorcing him. Since he was not living _____ any more, he _____ live in a hotel. Then, suddenly, he _____ the subway and walked away.

PART E   SUBSTITUTE THE CORRECT IDIOMS FOR THE BOLD FACE WORDS. THEN COPY THE WHOLE SENTENCE AND FINISH IT IN YOUR OWN WORDS.

1 Did you **accidentally meet** Henry while . . .? _____

2 Fred **enters** the bus at . . . . _____

3 Do you want to stay **in your house** or . . .? _____

4 I **must** study if . . . . _____

5 Before I **left** the plane in New York, I . . . . _____

_____

PART F   WRITE ONE PARAGRAPH ABOUT A FRIENDLY (AN UNFRIENDLY) NEIGHBOR. USE ALL FIVE IDIOMS.

COLORFUL IDIOM: **HIT THE NAIL ON THE HEAD.** Do or say whatever is exactly right.

test 1

A. DIRECTIONS

a Rearrange the letters in each box to make an idiom and write it in the box.

b Find the definition below that fits each idiom and put its *number* in the circle.

c Add the numbers in the circles across (→) or down (↓). The numbers must total 34 if your definitions are correct. To help you start, two answers were put in the boxes.

DEFINITIONS

1 starting now and continuing into the future; from this time forward
2 nothing more
3 alter my opinion; decide differently
4 go into, enter (a bus, train, plane, boat)
5 meet by chance
6 be a native of
7 gradually
8 What is wrong?
9 must, be obliged to
10 although
11 happen, occur
12 discard, throw away
13 give attention to
14 descend from, leave (a bus, train, plane, boat)
15 naturally
16 in your house

TA OMEH ⑯ _at home_	**NUR TOIN** ◯	**VAHE OT** ◯ ___	**EGT NO** ◯ ___	=34
TEG FOF ◯ ___	**SA CHUM SA** ◯ ___	**THAW SI HET TAMRET?** ◯ ___	**TAHT SI LAL** ◯ ___	=34
CEGNAH YM DIMN ◯ ___	**ELTILT YB ELTILT** ◯ ___	**OG NO** ◯ ___	**KEAT ARCE FO** ◯ ___	=34
MORF OWN NO ① _from now on_	**ETG DIR FO** ◯ ___	**MEOC ROMF** ◯ ___	**FO UROCSE** ◯ ___	=34
=34	=34	=34	=34	

MY NAME _____ TEACHER'S NAME _____ DATE _____

13

B FILL IN THE APPROPRIATE IDIOMS. USE EACH IDIOM ONLY ONCE, CHOOSING THE CORRECT TENSE AND PERSON.

from now on / have to / run into / change one's mind / come from / What's the matter?

1 When Carmen _____ Pedro at the store, she asked him,

2 " _____, Pedro? Is something wrong?"

3 Pedro answered: "I _____ buy some soap, but I can't find any."

4 Both Pedro and Carmen _____ Spain. But Pedro doesn't speak English very well.

5 _____, he is going to shop with Carmen. She'll help him.

C FROM PART E OF EXERCISES 1, 2, 3 YOUR INSTRUCTOR WILL READ ALOUD FIVE INCOMPLETE SENTENCES. COPY THEM DOWN. THEN DO AS YOU HAVE DONE BEFORE WITH PART E: SUBSTITUTE THE IDIOMS FROM THE LIST BELOW AND FINISH THE SENTENCES IN YOUR OWN WORDS. USE AN IDIOM ONLY ONCE.

that's all / take care of / little by little / get rid of / as much as / go on / get off / get on/ at home

1 _____

2 _____

3 _____

4 _____

5 _____

PROVERBS AND SAYINGS: **IF AT FIRST YOU DON'T SUCCEED, TRY, TRY AGAIN.**

exercise 4
Exchanging First Impressions of the United States

as many as
in the long run
see about
take a trip
take turns

MIMI: Sam, what was your first impression of the U. S.?

SAM: Just after I arrived here, I **took a trip** by bus from San Francisco to New York. All the open space between cities surprised me. The U. S. seemed almost without people.

MIMI: Your country is rather crowded, isn't it?

SAM: Yes, Japan has 50% of America's population but only 4% of its land. **As many as** 1100 people live on each square mile of land. But, Mimi, it's only fair we **take turns**. What was your first impression of the U. S.?

MIMI: A bad one. It was of American restaurants. I hated the food and I hated ice in my drinking water in January. That was the first thing my American waitress **saw about**—to put ice in my water.

SAM: I agree with you about the ice water. But what's so bad about American food?

MIMI: It's always the same. It's always hamburgers, fried chicken, or potatoes. And ice cream—even in winter. **In the long run**, it's bad for the stomach.

SAM: Aren't you exaggerating?

MIMI: I never exaggerate!

PART A   USING ALL FIVE IDIOMS, FILL IN THE BLANKS, ONE LETTER FOR EACH BLANK. MAKE EACH IDIOM AGREE IN TENSE AND PERSON WITH ITS SENTENCE.

Jill hates housework. She seldom / / / / / / / / / / / doing it before noon. / / / / / / / / / / four afternoons a week, she goes to the movies. Of course, she returns before her husband arrives home. Then she tells him how much work she has to do and he helps her. They even / / / / / / / / / / washing the dishes and ironing the clothes. She also avoids housework on weekends. Saturdays she / / / / / / / / / / / / to the next town and visits her friends. / / / / / / / / / / / / / / / she can avoid most of her housework by such methods.

PART B   SOME WORDS BELOW ARE BOLD FACE. SUBSTITUTE THE ABOVE IDIOMS WHICH MEAN THE SAME THING. THEN COPY THE COMPLETE SENTENCE IN THE SAME TENSE AND PERSON.

1 Watch our bags while Al **occupies himself with** the hotel bill._____

_____

2 **Finally** I'm going to be well again._____

MY NAME_____ TEACHER'S NAME_____ DATE_____

3 We both work, so we **alternate** cleaning the house. _____

_____

4 Phyllis **travels** to Miami every January. _____

5 **Equal to the number of** 25,000 people died in the Chicago fire of 1871. _____

_____

PART C   WRITE THE APPROPRIATE IDIOM. MAKE IT AGREE IN TENSE AND PERSON WITH THE REST OF THE SENTENCE.

Ruth and Martha lived on a farm. _____ three times a month, they had to _____ to a nearby town to buy food. While they were in town they_____ their groceries first. Then they went to visit friends. But they both really disliked shopping._____, it bored them. So they _____ carrying the groceries and driving the car. First one, then the other did it.

PART D   FILL IN THE BLANKS, USING ALL FIVE IDIOMS PLUS ONE FROM EXERCISE 3.

Oliver and his brother _____ to the United States last June. At first, they argued about which states to visit, but _____ they were able to agree. Before they started their trip, Oliver _____ the engine of their car. He checked it carefully. Both brothers could drive, so they _____ driving. They visited_____ ten states. On September 1, 1973, they _____ return home because they had no more money.

PART E   SUBSTITUTE THE CORRECT IDIOMS FOR THE BOLD FACE WORDS. THEN COPY THE WHOLE SENTENCE AND FINISH IT IN YOUR OWN WORDS.

1 **Finally** we are going to _____

2 This summer I'm **travelling** across _____

3 While you're fixing the car, I'll **occupy myself with** . . . . _____

_____

4 In World War II, **equal to the number of** . . . . _____

_____

5 Juan and Maria **alternate** . . . . _____

PART F   WRITE ONE PARAGRAPH ABOUT YOUR IMPRESSIONS OF THE U. S. (OR SOME OTHER COUNTRY). USE ALL FIVE IDIOMS.

COLORFUL IDIOM: **BEND SOMEONE'S EAR.** Talk excessively and continuously to a person.

exercise 5

Are Americans Impolite???

be used to
in fact
on the whole
right away
think of

MIMI: Americans aren't polite. **On the whole**, they're even impolite.

SAM: Really!

MIMI: Well, what do you **think of** strangers who call you by your first name? The day I moved into my apartment, the janitor came to fix the heating. **Right away** he called me Anne-Marie. And the next day the postman called me Annie. **In fact**, two minutes after they meet me, Americans begin inventing names for me.

SAM: But it's an American custom. They only mean to be friendly.

MIMI: We **are used to** politeness in France.

SAM: But customs are different in your country. Do you know that some Americans **think of** the French as unfriendly?

MIMI: They're idiots!

PART A   USING ALL FIVE IDIOMS, FILL IN THE BLANKS, ONE LETTER FOR EACH BLANK. MAKE EACH IDIOM AGREE IN TENSE AND PERSON WITH ITS SENTENCE.

Christine and Simone are pretty. When they go to a party, they meet young American men / / / / / / / / / / /. Because the men treat them politely, the two girls / / / / / / / / / / / politeness. Of course, they / / / / / / / / these men as friends and they like them. Yes, / / / / / / / / / / / / / / /, they like American men. / / / / / / / / /, they almost love them!

PART B   SOME WORDS BELOW ARE BOLD FACE. SUBSTITUTE THE ABOVE IDIOMS WHICH MEAN THE SAME THING. THEN COPY THE COMPLETE SENTENCE IN THE SAME TENSE AND PERSON.

1 I'm phoning my parents **immediately**. _____

2 Frank likes her very much; **really**, he loves her. _____

_____

3 I am **accustomed to** sleeping in the morning. _____

4 **In general**, Mimi is an excellent student. _____

5 What **is** Sam's **opinion** of her? _____

MY NAME_____ TEACHER'S NAME_____ DATE_____

PART C WRITE THE APPROPRIATE IDIOM. MAKE IT AGREE IN TENSE AND PERSON WITH THE REST OF THE SENTENCE.

Henri never wasted time. Whenever he went to an American supermarket he tried to find the fresh food _____ . Of course, his American friends were accustomed to eating frozen fish and vegetables, but he _____ eating fresh things.

What opinion did Henri have of American food? He _____ it as inferior to French food and he disliked most of it. Yes, _____ he disliked it. _____, he hated it!

PART D FILL IN THE BLANKS, USING ALL FIVE IDIOMS PLUS ONE FROM EXERCISE 4.

Sam is buying a Japanese car soon. _____, he's buying it tomorrow. Yesterday he examined _____ nine or ten cars, but _____ cars don't interest him. However, the minute he sees a Japanese car, he notices it. He notices it _____.

Does Mimi like Japanese cars? What does she _____ them? Of course, she likes them, but she prefers French cars. Why? Because she _____ them. She knows how to drive them.

PART E SUBSTITUTE THE CORRECT IDIOMS FOR THE BOLD FACE WORDS. THEN COPY THE WHOLE SENTENCE AND FINISH IT IN YOUR OWN WORDS.

1 My father left **immediately** because . . . . _____
2 Jim doesn't always tell the truth; **really**, he . . . . _____
_____
3 Sam **has an opinion of** Mimi as . . . . _____
4 **In general**, American women are . . . . _____
5 We **are accustomed to** drinking wine when . . . . _____
_____

PART F WRITE ONE PARAGRAPH ABOUT YOUR OPINION OF AMERICAN MANNERS. USE ALL FIVE IDIOMS.

COLORFUL IDIOM: **RAINING CATS AND DOGS.** Raining heavily.

exercise 6

A Country Where One O'Clock Means One O'Clock

had better
in time
on time
quite a few
talk (something) over [S] *

SAM: Aren't you ready, Mimi? The Browns' lunch is for one o'clock. We **had better** leave right away or we'll arrive late. They'll think we have bad manners.

MIMI: It isn't bad manners to be late. In France everybody's late.

SAM: In the U.S. everybody's **on time**. When lunch is for one p.m., your friends expect you at one p.m.

MIMI: Who said so?

SAM: My friends. I have a dozen or so American friends.

MIMI: That's **quite a few**.

SAM: They said it was bad manners to be late. We **talked** it **over**. So let's not be late.

MIMI: O.K. But first I have to fix my hair.

SAM: Oh no! We're going to arrive just **in time** for the end of the meal.

PART A   USING ALL FIVE IDIOMS, FILL IN THE BLANKS, ONE LETTER FOR EACH BLANK. MAKE EACH IDIOM AGREE IN TENSE AND PERSON WITH ITS SENTENCE.

Jack / / / / / / / / / / be at home when his mother phones or she'll be angry. She always phones him punctually at seven P.M. Since he knows that she always phones / / / / / / /, he does his best to arrive home / / / / / / / / to be there for her call.

Of course, they have / / / / / / / / / / / / things to say. Jack even tells her some of his problems and they / / / / / them / / / / /.

PART B   SOME WORDS BELOW ARE BOLD FACE. SUBSTITUTE THE ABOVE IDIOMS WHICH MEAN THE SAME THING. THEN COPY THE COMPLETE SENTENCE IN THE SAME TENSE AND PERSON.

1 You **should** wash your hands; they're dirty. _____

2 We have to arrive **punctually** at the doctor's office. _____

_____

3 I came home **early enough** to cook dinner. _____

4 **Many** of Mary's friends are mine. _____

* [S] indicates a separable idiom. A noun or pronoun may be inserted between its words.
  Example: TALK OVER [S]   We *talked over* our problems.
                               We *talked* them *over*.

MY NAME _____ TEACHER'S NAME _____ DATE_____

5 I **discussed** next summer's vacation with Phyllis. _____

_____

PART C   WRITE THE APPROPRIATE IDIOM. MAKE IT AGREE IN TENSE AND PERSON WITH THE REST OF THE SENTENCE.

Last week Joan's doctor _____ her health with her. He told her that if she wanted to get well quickly, she _____ do what he said. First, she had to go to bed _____ to get plenty of sleep. Second, she had to remember to take her medicine _____. She had to take it at exactly the right time. Finally, she could eat only certain things. There were _____ vegetables she couldn't eat.

PART D   FILL IN THE BLANKS, USING ALL FIVE IDIOMS PLUS ONE FROM EXERCISE 5.

MIMI: It's only two weeks until my American literature exam. I _____ begin to study if I want to be prepared _____ to do well on it. Of course, I know _____ books by American writers, but I don't know any by Hemingway. Can you _____ his books with me?

SAM: I can't do it now. I'm late for class. I have to leave_____.My English class begins at one o'clock and I want to get there _____.

PART E   SUBSTITUTE THE CORRECT IDIOMS FOR THE BOLD FACE WORDS. THEN COPY THE WHOLE SENTENCE AND FINISH IT IN YOUR OWN WORDS.

1   The train didn't arrive **punctually** because . . . . . _____

_____

2 **Many** of these jazz records belong . . . . _____

3 Did you come home **early enough** to . . .? _____

4 After **I discuss** my problems with my friends, I . . . . _____

_____

5 We **should** buy new tires for our car if . . . . _____

_____

PART F   WRITE ONE PARAGRAPH ABOUT THE TIME YOU WERE LATE (to class, to dinner, or to a party). USE ALL FIVE IDIOMS.

COLORFUL IDIOM: **HAVE A SWEET TOOTH.** Said of someone who likes sugar and candy very much.

test 2

A. DIRECTIONS

a Rearrange the letters in each box to make an idiom and write it in the box.

b Find the definition below that fits each idiom and put its *number* in the circle.

c Add the numbers in the circles across (——➤) or down (↓). The numbers must total 34.

DEFINITIONS

1 occupy yourself with
2 ought to, would be wise to
3 really, indeed
4 early enough
5 many, large number of
6 equal to the number of
7 finally, in the final outcome of
8 immediately
9 discuss
10 be accustomed to
11 have an opinion
12 go for a journey
13 in general
14 punctually, exactly at the fixed time
15 alternate
16 try really hard

KATE A PRIT ◯ ___	SA YAMN SA ◯ ___	KEAT SURNT ◯ ___	ESE UBOTA ◯ ___	=34
NI HET GLON NUR ◯ ___	NITHK FO ◯ ___	NO EHT LOHEW ◯ ___	NI CAFT ◯ ___	=34
EB DUSE OT ◯ ___	THIRG AYWA ◯ ___	DAH TEBERT ◯ ___	NO MITE ◯ ___	=34
ETUIQ A WEF ◯ ___	LAKT ORVE ◯ ___	NI METI ◯ ___	OD ROYU TEBS ◯ ___	=34
=34	=34	=34	=34	=34

MY NAME _____ DATE _____

TEACHER'S NAME _____

B   FILL IN THE APPROPRIATE IDIOMS. USE EACH IDIOM ONLY ONCE, CHOOSING THE CORRECT TENSE AND PRONOUN.

had better / take a trip / talk over / quite a few / right away / see about

1 Next week John and I plan to _____ to Europe.

2 In summer there are always _____ people who fly to Europe.

3 We should buy our plane tickets _____ or there may be none left.

4 John said he would _____ our tickets.

5 But I _____ make sure he doesn't forget.

C   FROM PART E OF EXERCISES 4, 5, 6 YOUR INSTRUCTOR WILL READ ALOUD FIVE INCOMPLETE SENTENCES. COPY THEM DOWN. THEN DO AS YOU HAVE DONE BEFORE WITH PART E: SUBSTITUTE THE IDIOMS FROM THE LIST BELOW AND FINISH THE SENTENCES IN YOUR OWN WORDS. USE AN IDIOM ONLY ONCE.

as many as / take turns / in the long run / think of / on the whole / in fact / be used to / on time / in time

1 _____

2 _____

3 _____

4 _____

5 _____

PROVERBS AND SAYINGS: **LOOK BEFORE YOU LEAP.**

exercise 7
Mimi Criticizes American Breakfasts

as well as
at (the) most
have a good time
(it's) no wonder
take advantage of

SAM: Over here, Mimi. I'm saving a seat for you.
MIMI: Please take my plate.
SAM: Is that all you're eating for breakfast?
MIMI: Yes, it is. French people never eat much in the morning—**at most** a cup of coffee and some bread.
SAM: Most Americans eat a big breakfast—bacon, eggs, two or three pieces of toast **as well as** cereal and coffee.
MIMI: **(It's) no wonder** their TV is always selling them medicine for sick stomachs.
SAM: Mimi, you're terrible! You're always **taking advantage of** something to criticize Americans.
MIMI: And I **have a good time** doing it. It amuses me.

PART A USING ALL FIVE IDIOMS, FILL IN THE BLANKS, ONE LETTER FOR EACH BLANK. MAKE EACH IDIOM AGREE IN TENSE AND PERSON WITH ITS SENTENCE.

Carl earns only $50 a week. Because he has to pay for his apartment /_/_/_/_/_/_/_/_/_/ (for) his clothes, he can spend /_/_/_/_/_/_/ $15 a week on food. That's why he is always /_/_/_/_/_/_/_/_/_/_/_/_/_/ sales to save money.

Rich people travel, go to parties and /_/_/_/_/_/_/_/_/_/_/_/_/_/_/_/ . Poor people do not. /_/_/_/_/_/_/_/_/ Carl wants to be rich.

PART B SOME WORDS BELOW ARE BOLD FACE. SUBSTITUTE THE ABOVE IDIOMS WHICH MEAN THE SAME THING. THEN COPY THE COMPLETE SENTENCE IN THE SAME TENSE AND PERSON.

1 Every morning I run two miles or **a maximum of** three. _____

_____

2 He's forever eating candy; **it's not surprising** he's fat. _____

_____

3 John gave his wife a gold watch **in addition to** a diamond. _____

_____

4 I'm **profiting from** free time to play golf. _____

5 I'm **enjoying myself** watching TV. _____

PART C WRITE THE APPROPRIATE IDIOM. MAKE IT AGREE IN TENSE AND PERSON WITH THE REST OF THE SENTENCE.

Irene wanted to be thin, so she ate _____ one egg for breakfast. She hoped to lose weight from her stomach _____ (from) her legs. By _____ a nearby lake, she was able to swim regularly. She also hoped to lose a few pounds that way.

Thin people ate what they liked, went to good restaurants and _____, but Irene did not. _____ that she wanted to be thin.

PART D FILL IN THE BLANKS, USING ALL FIVE IDIOMS PLUS ONE FROM EXERCISE 6.

There are _____ sports I like. For example, I enjoy skiing _____ swimming and golf. I also _____ sailing, so I try to _____ my summer vacation to sail my boat. However, I get only a week or, _____, ten days vacation. _____ I spend ten hours a day in my boat.

PART E SUBSTITUTE THE CORRECT IDIOMS FOR THE BOLD FACE WORDS. THEN COPY THE WHOLE SENTENCE AND FINISH IT IN YOUR OWN WORDS.

1 Jack is **profiting from** his knowledge of English . . . . _____

_____

2 Since you don't save your money, **it's not surprising** that . . . . _____

_____

3 I can eat **a maximum of** . . . . _____

4 Bill is **enjoying himself** . . . . _____

5 Did Frank buy a glass of milk **in addition to** . . . . _____

_____

PART F WRITE ONE PARAGRAPH ABOUT BREAKFAST IN YOUR NATIVE LAND. USE ALL FIVE IDIOMS.

COLORFUL IDIOM: **FULL OF THE DEVIL.** Often said of mischievous children.

exercise 8

More Impressions of the United States: Freezing in Summer; Boiling in Winter

catch cold
find fault with
put on [S]
think (something) over [S]
time after time

MIMI: The weather is getting hot. I'll have to **put on** my sweater.
SAM: ??????
MIMI: It's because of American air conditioning.
SAM: Oh?
MIMI: All the buildings have it. They're really cool inside. Two minutes after I go in, I start shaking. Then I **catch cold**.
SAM: It's American heating that makes me unhappy. All winter my office is at 75 degrees. Everyone but me likes it that way.
MIMI: Do you suppose that's why Americans wear lightweight clothes—to stay cool in winter?
SAM: If you **think** it **over**, that has to be the reason. Say, maybe they ought to wear bathing suits in winter.
MIMI: Sam, you mustn't **find fault with** Americans. Isn't that what you tell me **time after time**?
SAM: You're right! Even if they freeze us in summer and boil us in winter, they're nice people.

PART A   USING ALL FIVE IDIOMS, FILL IN THE BLANKS, ONE LETTER FOR EACH BLANK. MAKE EACH IDIOM AGREE IN TENSE AND PERSON WITH ITS SENTENCE.

In Boston, people think the winters are terrible, and they /_/_/_/_/_/_/_/_/_/_/_/ /_/_/_/_/_/ the freezing weather. Of course, my wife and I /_/_/_/_/_/_/ our warmest clothes. But it doesn't help. Six or seven times a winter we /_/_/_/_/_/_/_/_/_/_/. We get sick /_/_/_/_/_/_/_/_/_/_/_/_/_/_/_/_/. "What can we do?" we ask ourselves. We /_/_/_/_/_/_/ it /_/_/_/_/ and decide to move to Florida.

PART B   SOME WORDS BELOW ARE BOLD FACE. SUBSTITUTE THE ABOVE IDIOMS WHICH MEAN THE SAME THING. THEN COPY THE COMPLETE SENTENCE IN THE SAME TENSE AND PERSON.

1 I ask him **again and again** to drive carefully. _____

2 Wear your winter coat today or you'll **become ill with a cold**. _____

_____

3 Let Bill **consider** the matter **carefully**; he can give me an answer Friday. _____

_____

MY NAME _____ TEACHER'S NAME _____ DATE _____

4 When Suzy cleans her house, she **wears** old clothes. _____

_____

5 I do my best. Why do you always **criticize** my work? _____

_____

PART C   WRITE THE APPROPRIATE IDIOM. MAKE IT AGREE IN TENSE AND PERSON WITH THE REST OF THE SENTENCE.

Jim _____ at work and became sick. But he didn't go to a doctor. Instead, he did some thinking first. He _____ the various ways to treat a cold. Then he _____ his hat and coat, went home and drank a bottle of whiskey. When his wife saw what he was doing, she got angry and _____ him. "You're always drinking whiskey," she shouted. "You get drunk _____."

PART D   FILL IN THE BLANKS, USING ALL FIVE IDIOMS PLUS ONE FROM EXERCISE 7.

Tom loves sales. Last January he _____ a clothing sale to buy some neckties at a low price. But before he bought them, he _____ each tie and looked at himself in a mirror. Was this the right one for him? He carefully _____ what he should buy.

However, Tom's wife was unhappy with him. She _____ the ties he bought. "Besides," she said, "going in and out of stores in winter is a good way to _____. You get sick this way _____."

PART E   SUBSTITUTE THE CORRECT IDIOMS FOR THE BOLD FACE WORDS. THEN COPY THE WHOLE SENTENCE AND FINISH IT IN YOUR OWN WORDS.

1 Henry failed **again and again** to . . . . _____

2 Before I go into a store, I **consider carefully** what . . . . _____

_____

3 I'm always **criticizing** my friends because . . . . _____

_____

4 Billy **becomes ill with a cold** when . . . . _____

5 To go to the movies, I **wear** . . . . _____

PART F   WRITE ONE PARAGRAPH ABOUT THE LAST TIME YOU WERE SICK. USE ALL FIVE IDIOMS.

COLORFUL IDIOM: **HIT THE CEILING.** Suddenly become very angry; explode with anger.

exercise 9

Why Didn't God Build
American Women Differently?

bring up [S]
find out [S]
give up [S]
how's that?
on the other hand

MIMI: I **give up** trying to understand Americans. They're always surprising me.
SAM: **How's that?**
MIMI: Well, I **found out** that millions of Americans buy books that teach them good manners.
SAM: Now that you **bring up** the subject—yes, I discovered the same thing.
MIMI: **On the other hand**, lots of Americans act as if manners didn't exist. The men wear sportshirts to church. The women wear curlers while they drive around the city. Or pants while they're walking about.
SAM: Are you saying that American women can't wear pants and have good manners?
MIMI: That's right. Besides, if God wanted women to wear pants, He would build them differently.

PART A   USING ALL FIVE IDIOMS, FILL IN THE BLANKS, ONE LETTER FOR EACH BLANK. MAKE EACH IDIOM AGREE IN TENSE AND PERSON WITH ITS SENTENCE.

Why did I / / / / / / / drinking wine? Because I / / / / / / / / / that it was bad for my stomach. / / / / / / / / / / / / / / / / / /, it was good for my nerves. In the past, whenever my wife / / / / / / / / / / / the idea of buying a new dress, I always drank another glass of wine and said smilingly, "I'll think about it."

"/ / / ' / / / / /?" she would ask. "Do you mean yes or no?"

PART B   SOME WORDS BELOW ARE BOLD FACE. SUBSTITUTE THE ABOVE IDIOMS WHICH MEAN THE SAME THING. THEN COPY THE COMPLETE SENTENCE IN THE SAME TENSE AND PERSON.

1 I don't **raise** subjects which make my boss angry. _____

_____

2 I like to visit the U.S. **From the opposite viewpoint**, I prefer living in Spain._____

_____

3 Richard **stopped** riding horses after he broke his back. _____

_____

4 I hope he **discovers** who stole my car. _____

5 **Can you explain?** I don't think I heard correctly. _____

MY NAME _____ TEACHER'S NAME _____ DATE _____

PART C WRITE THE APPROPRIATE IDIOM. MAKE IT AGREE IN TENSE AND PERSON WITH THE REST OF THE SENTENCE.

Why did Peggy _____ smoking. Because she _____ that it hurt her lungs. _____, it kept her thin: she smoked a cigarette rather than ate dessert. But now when her husband _____ the subject of dessert, she always says yes. He is surprised because he never knew she liked it. "_____ ?" he asks her.

PART D FILL IN THE BLANKS, USING ALL FIVE IDIOMS PLUS ONE FROM EXERCISE 8.

Because my son was lazy, I often _____ him and criticized him severely. For example, if he didn't know an answer, he soon _____ trying to find it. _____, my wife wasn't lazy. If she couldn't _____ something at home, she put on her coat and went to the library. Or she _____ it _____ with friends and asked them. When the question was too difficult, they replied, "_____? We don't understand what you want to know."

PART E SUBSTITUTE THE CORRECT IDIOMS FOR THE BOLD FACE WORDS. THEN COPY THE WHOLE SENTENCE AND FINISH IT IN YOUR OWN WORDS.

1 **"Can you explain?"** I ask, when . . . . _____

2 When Jack **discovers** his mistake, he will . . . . _____
_____

3 Janet **stopped** eating candy before . . . . _____

4 (I like the way people live in Russia.) **From the opposite viewpoint**, I don't like . . . . _____
_____

5 Her husband **raises** the question of money each time . . . . _____
_____

PART F WRITE ONE PARAGRAPH ABOUT THE ADVANTAGES OF BEING A WOMAN (MAN). USE ALL FIVE IDIOMS.

COLORFUL IDIOM: **SPLIT YOUR SIDES LAUGHING.** Laugh long and hard.

test 3

A. DIRECTIONS

a Rearrange the letters in each box to make an idiom and write it in the box.

b Find the definition below that fits each idiom and put its *number* in the circle.

c Add the numbers in the circles across (⟶) or down (↓). The numbers must total 34.

EVAH A DOGO MITE ◯ ___	AKET GEATVAND FO ◯ ___	ON NOWRED ◯ ___	SA LEWL SA ◯ ___ =34
TA OSMT ◯ ___	DINF FULAT TIWH ◯ ___	INTKH REVO ◯ ___	TUP NO ◯ ___ =34
CHATC DOLC ◯ ___	IMET ERFAT IMET ◯ ___	GRINB PU ◯ ___	EVGI PU ◯ ___ =34
NO TEH TOHER DANH ◯ ___	DINF OTU ◯ ___	OWH SI TATH? ◯ ___	TEG MIDEX PU ◯ ___ =34
=34	=34	=34	=34

DEFINITIONS

1 confused
2 no more than, a maximum of
3 renounce, abandon
4 enjoy yourself
5 use profitably
6 Can you explain?
7 continually, again and again
8 consider carefully
9 it is not surprising
10 criticize
11 raise or present a question
12 learn, discover
13 become ill with a cold
14 wear, dress in
15 from the opposite point of view
16 in addition to

MY NAME _____

TEACHER'S NAME _____ DATE _____

29

B FILL IN THE APPROPRIATE IDIOMS. USE EACH IDIOM ONLY ONCE, CHOOSING THE CORRECT TENSE AND PRONOUN.

think over / no wonder / find fault with / put on / catch cold / give up

1 Ingrid hates to carry an umbrella. She doesn't _____ a raincoat either.

2 _____ she becomes ill so often.

3 Yesterday she _____. She began to sneeze and cough.

4 Ingrid's mother was unhappy about her. She often _____ her daughter.

5 But Ingrid never listened and her mother finally _____ warning her.

C FROM PART E OF EXERCISES 7, 8, 9 YOUR INSTRUCTOR WILL READ ALOUD FIVE INCOMPLETE SENTENCES. COPY THEM DOWN. THEN DO AS YOU HAVE DONE BEFORE WITH PART E: SUBSTITUTE THE IDIOMS FROM THE LIST BELOW AND FINISH THE SENTENCES IN YOUR OWN WORDS. USE AN IDIOM ONLY ONCE.

have a good time / take advantage of / as well as / at most / time after time / bring up / on the other hand / find out / How's that? / Have a good time

1 _____

2 _____

3 _____

4 _____

5 _____

PROVERBS AND SAYINGS: **WHATEVER IS WORTH DOING IS WORTH DOING WELL.**

exercise 10

Heart Attacks:
the American Way of Death

as for
in a hurry
make sense
put in [S]
What about . . . ?

MIMI: Why do so many Americans have heart attacks?

SAM: Because they're always **in a hurry**. They just can't relax.

MIMI: Do you really believe that?

SAM: Well, my doctor says that Americans eat like pigs and smoke like chimneys. But they don't exercise and they don't know how to relax. That's why they have heart attacks.

MIMI: And Sally's father?

SAM: ????????

MIMI: He didn't smoke, ate like a bird and played golf three times a week. So why did he have a heart attack? It doesn't **make sense**.

SAM: **As for** him, he was very nervous. Besides, he worked too hard. He **put in** sixty hours a week at his job.

MIMI: I feel tired. **What about** taking me home early tonight?

PART A   USING ALL FIVE IDIOMS, FILL IN THE BLANKS, ONE LETTER FOR EACH BLANK. MAKE EACH IDIOM AGREE IN TENSE AND PERSON WITH ITS SENTENCE.

BOB: A hard job makes me hungry. / / / / / / / / / / / / (eating) a hamburger?

AL: Maybe that's okay for you, Bob. / / / / / / / me, I don't like hamburgers.

BOB: Do you like hot dogs? We can eat them / / / / / / / / / / / and relax a few minutes before our next job.

AL: I hate hot dogs! But I'm so hungry it / / / / / / / / / / / / to eat a hot dog.

BOB: Good! Now let's / / / / / / / a few minutes eating and relaxing.

PART B   SOME WORDS BELOW ARE BOLD FACE. SUBSTITUTE THE ABOVE IDIOMS WHICH MEAN THE SAME THING. THEN COPY THE COMPLETE SENTENCE IN THE SAME TENSE AND PERSON.

1 **How would you like** going to a good movie? _____

2 It **seems reasonable** to save one's money. _____

3 We **spent** a whole day studying at the library. _____

4 We have to leave now; we're **pressed for time**. _____

5 **With reference to** English, I like it very much. _____

MY NAME _____ TEACHER'S NAME _____ DATE _____

PART C   WRITE THE APPROPRIATE IDIOM. MAKE IT AGREE IN TENSE AND PERSON WITH THE REST OF THE SENTENCE.

JANE: A rainy evening makes me sad. _____ (going to) a movie?

HENRY: Perhaps that's fine for you, Jane. _____ me, I hate movies.

JANE: Do you want to stay here? I can see that you're not _____ to leave.

HENRY: Rather than stay here, it does _____ to go to a movie.

JANE: Wonderful! We can even _____ a half hour studying before we leave.

PART D   FILL IN THE BLANKS, USING ALL FIVE IDIOMS PLUS ONE FROM EXERCISE 9.

Why was Joe driving so fast when his car hit mine? I _____ the reason afterwards. He was _____ to get his wife to the hospital.

Of course, my car was badly damaged. _____ his, it had only a broken headlight. Still it didn't _____ for him to drive that fast. He will have to _____ weeks of work to pay for my damages. That's why I always say no when my friends ask me, "_____ driving a little faster?"

PART E   SUBSTITUTE THE CORRECT IDIOMS FOR THE BOLD FACE WORDS. THEN COPY THE WHOLE SENTENCE AND FINISH IT IN YOUR OWN WORDS.

1 **With reference to** the money I owe you, I . . . . _____

2 Students are always **pressed for time** . . . . _____

3 Colette **spends** her weekends . . . . _____

4 When my son was sick, it **seemed reasonable** to . . . . _____
_____

5 **How would you like** coming . . . ? _____

PART F   WRITE ONE PARAGRAPH ABOUT HOW MUCH (LITTLE) YOU STUDY. USE ALL FIVE IDIOMS.

COLORFUL IDIOM: **PUSHING UP DAISIES.** Said of someone who is dead and buried.

exercise 11
The Sex-Mad Americans

all right
at all
do without
go too far
have (someone) over [S]

MIMI: Sex! Sex! Sex! That's all Americans talk or read about!

SAM: **Aren't** you **going too far**?

MIMI: Every time they **have** me **over** we spend the evening talking about sex. In France we know it exists, but we read and talk about other things.

SAM: Do you? Some of your greatest authors—de Beauvoir, Sagan, Aymé—wrote about sex. And Frenchmen are still buying their books, aren't they?

MIMI: **All right**, I admit it. But have you seen the new American movies?

SAM: They're full of sex, I agree. But some French movies are not **at all** for children or little old ladies.

MIMI: Sam. . .why do you attack the French each time I find fault with Americans?

SAM: I was only joking.

MIMI: I can **do without** your jokes.

PART A   USING ALL FIVE IDIOMS, FILL IN THE BLANKS, ONE LETTER FOR EACH BLANK. MAKE EACH IDIOM AGREE IN TENSE AND PERSON WITH ITS SENTENCE.

Once a week Mimi invites Sam to her apartment. She / / / / / / / / / / / / / for dinner. At the end of the meal she always serves him wine and cheese. "If we eat cheese," she tells him, "we can / / / / / / / / / / / milk." Then she asks him what he would like to eat next week: "Is it / / / / / / / / / / / if I serve you another French dish?" Sam agrees right away; he doesn't object / / / / / / / to good French cooking. It isn't / / / / / / / / / / / / / / / / to say he *loves* Mimi's cooking.

PART B   SOME WORDS BELOW ARE BOLD FACE. SUBSTITUTE THE ABOVE IDIOMS WHICH MEAN THE SAME THING. THEN COPY THE COMPLETE SENTENCE IN THE SAME TENSE AND PERSON.

1 He isn't **in the least** sure she's going with him. _____

_____

2 It's **passing beyond a certain limit** to walk around naked. _____

_____

3 It's **O.K.** with me if we leave right away. _____

4 Some people can **omit** sleeping. _____

MY NAME _____ TEACHER'S NAME _____ DATE _____

5 Tomorrow I'm **inviting** my whole family to lunch. _____

PART C   WRITE THE APPROPRIATE IDIOM. MAKE IT AGREE IN TENSE AND PERSON WITH THE REST OF THE SENTENCE.

Sam told Mimi that the French _____ recently in forbidding certain films. She told him that he was stupid and walked off.

But Sam liked Mimi so much that he couldn't _____ her. The very next day he invited her to his house for lunch.

"Is it _____ to bring a friend with me?" she asked

Sam wasn't _____ eager to have another guest, but he politely said yes and

_____ the two girls _____ for lunch.

PART D   FILL IN THE BLANKS, USING ALL FIVE IDIOMS PLUS ONE FROM EXERCISE 10.

It is not _____ unusual for Americans to have many friends and to invite them into their homes. They especially like to _____ for dinner. If you are a guest, you may phone ahead of time and ask, "Is it _____ if I wear a sports shirt?" Usually you can wear what you wish, but it is _____ if you come in a bathing suit. On the whole, American customs are reasonable; they _____ . Besides, even Americans cannot _____ them.

PART E   SUBSTITUTE THE CORRECT IDIOMS FOR THE BOLD FACE WORDS. THEN COPY THE WHOLE SENTENCE AND FINISH IT IN YOUR OWN WORDS.

1 Is it **O.K.** with you if . . . ? _____

2 Harry **passed beyond a certain limit** when . . . . _____

3 I'm **inviting** some friends tomorrow to . . . . _____

_____

4 Betty **omitted** lunch yesterday because . . . . _____

_____

5 We aren't **in the least** unhappy that . . . . _____

PART F   WRITE ONE PARAGRAPH ABOUT AN EVENING YOU SPENT WITH FRIENDS. USE ALL FIVE IDIOMS.

COLORFUL IDIOM: **LADY KILLER.** A man exceptionally successful with women.

exercise 12
Finding
A Job

all day long
call on
for the time being
make a living
sooner or later

MIMI: Is it difficult to **make a living** in the U. S.?
SAM: No. The average American factory worker earns $7.82 an hour.
MIMI: And secretaries—how much do they earn?
SAM: As much as $7.13 an hour. But why do you want to know?
MIMI: Because I have a friend who needs money. **For the time being** she has enough to pay her bills. But **sooner or later** she must find a job.
SAM: When does she want to start working?
MIMI: Right away. Yesterday she spent **all day long** phoning. But no one wanted a secretary.
SAM: Maybe I can help her. I'm **calling on** some American friends tomorrow. I can mention her name during the visit.

PART A USING ALL FIVE IDIOMS, FILL IN THE BLANKS, ONE LETTER FOR EACH BLANK. MAKE EACH IDIOM AGREE IN TENSE AND PERSON WITH ITS SENTENCE.

Jan ⌐/ / / / / /⌐/ / / / / / /⌐ as a secretary. She earns enough money to pay her rent, food and clothes. ⌐/ / /⌐ /⌐ / / / /⌐ / / / / / / / /⌐ she has everything she really needs.

⌐/ / / / / / / /⌐ / / / /⌐ / / / /⌐, however, she is going to want a better job. Then she will have to visit the big companies and ⌐/ / / /⌐/ / /⌐ some businessmen personally. Or she can stay at home and telephone them. She can telephone ⌐/ / / /⌐/ / / /⌐ / / /⌐. They will be in their offices the whole day.

PART B SOME WORDS BELOW ARE BOLD FACE. SUBSTITUTE THE ABOVE IDIOMS WHICH MEAN THE SAME THING. THEN COPY THE COMPLETE SENTENCE IN THE SAME TENSE AND PERSON.

1 **Temporarily** I am feeling better. _____

2 In some countries people can't **earn enough money to live adequately**. _____

_____

3 I'm going to become rich **eventually**. _____

4 Jane was happy; she sang **the whole day**. _____

5 The priest **visited** my family yesterday. _____

MY NAME _____ TEACHER'S NAME _____ DATE _____

PART C WRITE THE APPROPRIATE IDIOM. MAKE IT AGREE IN TENSE AND PERSON WITH THE REST OF THE SENTENCE.

Jim earned enough money to provide for the needs of his family. For years he _____ repairing TV sets. "_____ we have enough money," he told his wife. "But in September we'll be moving to a larger house. _____ we're going to need more money. I'll have to find a better job."

Yesterday Jim took a trip to Chicago to find a job. He _____ quite a few TV repair shops there. And _____ today he was writing job applications.

PART D FILL IN THE BLANKS, USING ALL FIVE IDIOMS PLUS ONE FROM EXERCISE 11.

As a salesman, Bill worked many hours a day to _____. In fact, he worked _____ . He _____ hundreds of people and talked to them in their homes. This week Bill isn't feeling _____ well. _____, he must stay in bed and rest. But _____ he is going to return to work. Perhaps tomorrow. Perhaps next week.

PART E SUBSTITUTE THE CORRECT IDIOMS FOR THE BOLD FACE WORDS. THEN COPY THE WHOLE SENTENCE AND FINISH IT IN YOUR OWN WORDS.

1 We are living in Los Angeles **temporarily**, but we hope to . . . . _____

_____

2 Did Matthew **visit** Sally when . . . ? _____

3 I worked **the whole day** before . . . . _____

4 Everyone knows that Mary is going to . . . . **eventually**. _____

_____

5 Can the average man **earn enough to live adequately** if . . . ? _____

_____

PART F WRITE ONE PARAGRAPH ABOUT FINDING A JOB. USE ALL FIVE IDIOMS.

COLORFUL IDIOM: **LOSE YOUR HEAD.** Lose your self-control; become excited or flustered.

test 4

A. DIRECTIONS

a   Rearrange the letters in each box to make an idiom and write it in the box.

b   Find the definition below that fits each idiom and put its *number* in the circle.

c   Add the numbers in the circles across (——→) or down (↓). The numbers must total 34.

DEFINITIONS

1   early
2   temporarily
3   with reference to
4   invite
5   to spend time in a specified manner
6   the entire day
7   How would you like. . .?
8   in the least
9   pass beyond a certain limit
10   okay; satisfactory
11   with a need to act quickly, rushed
12   visit
13   be logical
14   inevitably; ultimately
15   earn enough to live adequately
16   manage without, live without something

TWAH TABOU ○ ___	NI A RYHUR ○ ___	KEAM ESSEN ○ ___	SA ORF ○ ___
TUP NI ○ ___	OG OTO ARF ○ ___	VAHE ROVE ○ ___	OD TOUTHIW ○ ___
LAL THIRG ○ ___	TA LAL ○ ___	ROF TEH MITE BINGE ○ ___	ONOSER RO TELAR ○ ___
LACL NO ○ ___	LAL ADY NOLG ○ ___	EKMA A INGVIL ○ ___	ADEHA FO MEIT ○ ___

MY NAME _____ TEACHER'S NAME _____ DATE _____

38

B FILL IN THE APPROPRIATE IDIOMS. USE EACH IDIOM ONLY ONCE, CHOOSING THE CORRECT TENSE AND PRONOUN.

do without / as for / make a living / sooner or later / put in / all day long

1 To _____, I work at the library.

2 Everyday I work there _____ .

3 I _____ 45 hours a week.

4 I usually _____ my lunch hour to finish work earlier.

5 _____ my boyfriend, he isn't too happy. I don't have much time to see him.

C FROM PART E OF EXERCISES 10, 11, 12 YOUR INSTRUCTOR WILL READ ALOUD FIVE INCOMPLETE SENTENCES. COPY THEM DOWN. THEN DO AS YOU HAVE DONE BEFORE WITH PART E: SUBSTITUTE THE IDIOMS FROM THE LIST BELOW AND FINISH THE SENTENCES IN YOUR OWN WORDS. USE AN IDIOM ONLY ONCE.

What about. . . ? / In a hurry / make sense / go too far / have over / all right / call on / for the time being / at all

1 _____

2 _____

3 _____

4 _____

5 _____

PROVERBS AND SAYINGS: **MAKE HASTE SLOWLY.**

exercise 13
Why Americans Build Skyscrapers

all the time
as far as
get back
in the first place
used to

SAM: Did you just **get back** from New York?

MIMI: Yes, at nine this morning.

SAM: Tell me: What did you think of the skyscrapers there?

MIMI: **As far as** I could judge, they were horrible.

SAM: Why?

MIMI: **In the first place**, they were too high. The sunlight couldn't reach the streets below. This made shopping in Manhattan like walking down one long, dark corridor after another. In the second place, I felt **all the time** that they were going to fall on me.

SAM: Do you know why Americans build skyscrapers?

MIMI: To make me unhappy?

SAM: No, silly. At first, only a few farmers **used to** live on Manhattan Island. Then little by little it became a center of trade. There were millions of people, thousands of businesses, but not enough space. The only space left was between the ground and the sky. Skyscrapers solved the space problem. They still do.

PART A   USING ALL FIVE IDIOMS, FILL IN THE BLANKS, ONE LETTER FOR EACH BLANK. MAKE EACH IDIOM AGREE IN TENSE AND PERSON WITH ITS SENTENCE.

I / / / / / / / think people worked hard. I was wrong. / / / / / / / / / I can judge, they don't work hard at all. /, they don't realize that success requires work. In the second place, they don't save their money. Of course, some people work very hard, and a few of them work / / / / / / / / / / / / /. They even work too much. When they / / / / / / / / / home at night, they are tired and nervous.

PART B   SOME WORDS BELOW ARE BOLD FACE. SUBSTITUTE THE ABOVE IDIOMS WHICH MEAN THE SAME THING. THEN COPY THE COMPLETE SENTENCE IN THE SAME TENSE AND PERSON.

1 **To the extent that** I could judge, Mimi spoke good English. _____

_____

2 Ray gets good grades; he is studying **continually**. _____

_____

3 I **continued for some time to** drive a taxi. _____

MY NAME _____ TEACHER'S NAME _____ DATE _____

40

4 **To begin with**, I don't have the time to go with you. _____

_____

5 I **returned** from Sally's at ten. _____

PART C   WRITE THE APPROPRIATE IDIOM. MAKE IT AGREE IN TENSE AND PERSON WITH THE REST OF THE SENTENCE.

I _____ think the men in my office were intelligent. _____ I can tell now, I was mistaken. Most of them weren't intelligent at all. _____, they didn't know that thinking required effort. In the second place, they didn't have good minds. Only a few men were intelligent. They were thinking _____. In fact, they thought too much. At night, when they _____ they often had a headache.

PART D   FILL IN THE BLANKS, USING ALL FIVE IDIOMS PLUS ONE FROM EXERCISE 12.

Mimi is in New York. _____ she is staying at the Hotel Regent._____ she knows now, she doesn't have to _____ until next week.

In the past Mimi _____ have a good time in New York. Why? _____, there was lots to see and do. She could enjoy herself _____. Second, she had quite a few friends there.

PART E   SUBSTITUTE THE CORRECT IDIOMS FOR THE BOLD FACE WORDS. THEN COPY THE WHOLE SENTENCE AND FINISH IT IN YOUR OWN WORDS.

1 Olga **returned** from New York. . . ._____
2 (Perhaps we can find out why George gets bad grades.) **To begin with**, he . . . ._____

_____

3 My father **continued for some time to** . . . . _____
4 I go to the movies **continually** because . . . . _____
5 **To the extent that** I know, my sister. . . . _____

PART F   WRITE ONE PARAGRAPH ABOUT YOUR FAVORITE CITY. USE ALL FIVE IDIOMS.

COLORFUL IDIOM: **MAKE YOUR HAIR STAND ON END.** Something sufficient to terrify you.

exercise 14
TV: For Kids
and Idiots Only?

keep up with
make a point of
put up with
turn off [S]
turn on [S]

MIMI: I **make a point of** avoiding American TV. It's for kids and idiots.

SAM: I don't agree. The TV news is very adult. I **turn** it **on** every night at 6:30. It gives me facts. It tells me what's going on. It helps me **keep up with** the world.

MIMI: The news lasts thirty minutes. What do you think you're watching the rest of the day? Great ideas?

SAM: Well, there are also educational programs—you know, programs about art and science.

MIMI: They're fine if you can **put up with** five minutes of advertising for ten minutes of program. As for me, I **turn off** the sound whenever there's an advertisement.

SAM: That's un-American!

PART A   USING ALL FIVE IDIOMS, FILL IN THE BLANKS, ONE LETTER FOR EACH BLANK. MAKE EACH IDIOM AGREE IN TENSE AND PERSON WITH ITS SENTENCE.

Jack hates the movies, so he / / / / / / / / / / / / / / / / / / never going. He also hates TV, but he / / / / / / / / / / / / / / / it because he likes to watch the news. Five minutes before the news, he / / / / / / / / / his TV set. The minute the news ends, he / / / / / / / / / / / / / again. However, he does like to read. He reads all the recent books and he / / / / / / / / / / / / / / / the latest magazines.

PART B   SOME WORDS BELOW ARE BOLD FACE. SUBSTITUTE THE ABOVE IDIOMS WHICH MEAN THE SAME THING. THEN COPY THE COMPLETE SENTENCE IN THE SAME TENSE AND PERSON.

1 It was my wife who **stopped the operation of** the gas oven. _____

_____

2 My neighbor **started the operation of** his record player at midnight. _____

_____

3 She **insists upon** driving her husband to work. _____

_____

4 Tell the kids to go outside: I can't **tolerate** their noise any longer. _____

_____

MY NAME _____ TEACHER'S NAME _____ DATE _____

5 Carol tries to **stay informed of** what her friends are doing. _____

_____

PART C   WRITE THE APPROPRIATE IDIOM. MAKE IT AGREE IN TENSE AND PERSON WITH THE REST OF THE SENTENCE.

Bob loved the movies, so he _____ going twice a week. He enjoyed the old Charlie Chaplin films. But he also liked to see the new films, and he _____ what was new on TV, too.

On the other hand, Bob's wife hated movies, but she _____ them because she wanted to spend her evenings with her husband. On the nights she stayed at home alone, she felt afraid. She _____ all the lights in the house. She _____ only when Bob got back.

PART D   FILL IN THE BLANKS, USING ALL FIVE IDIOMS PLUS ONE FROM EXERCISE 13.

As a salesman, I was always successful because I _____ today's ideas. In fact, I _____ asking other salesmen about new ideas, and once or twice a month I _____ call on them. Unfortunately, they weren't like radios. I couldn't _____ when I wanted to listen to them and _____ when I didn't, so I had to _____ a lot of stupid talk.

PART E   SUBSTITUTE THE CORRECT IDIOMS FOR THE BOLD FACE WORDS. THEN COPY THE WHOLE SENTENCE AND FINISH IT IN YOUR OWN WORDS.

1 Last summer my father **stopped the operation of** all the water in the house and .... _____

_____

2 (It was cold last night.) I **started the operation of** .... _____

_____

3 Henry will **tolerate** Elizabeth's bad manners until .... _____

_____

4 Juan **insisted upon** telling .... _____

5 I **stay informed of** what's going on in .... _____

PART F   WRITE ONE PARAGRAPH ABOUT THE TV PROGRAM YOU LIKE BEST (LEAST). USE ALL FIVE IDIOMS.

COLORFUL IDIOM: **I COULD KICK MYSELF.** A person often says this when he misses a good opportunity and blames himself.

exercise 15
Mimi Decides
to go Skiing

as usual
at least
look forward to
make sure
make the most of

SAM: I'm **looking forward to** my Christmas vacation.
MIMI: So am I. I try to **make the most of** the few days I have. What are you going to do?
SAM: **As usual**, I'm going skiing. I go every year.
MIMI: And if there's no snow. . . ?
SAM: I hope for **at least** an inch of snow. It depends on the weather at Stowe.
MIMI: You mean, Stowe, Vermont?
SAM: That's right. Why do you ask?
MIMI: To **make sure** we're going to the same place. I mean, I'm skiing there this Christmas, too.
SAM: Wonderful! We can go skiing together.

PART A USING ALL FIVE IDIOMS, FILL IN THE BLANKS, ONE LETTER FOR EACH BLANK. MAKE EACH IDIOM AGREE IN TENSE AND PERSON WITH ITS SENTENCE.

Pierre and Jerome never save their money. ⌊_⌋_⌊_⌋_⌊_⌋_⌊_⌋, their father is sending them the money for their rent. In this way he ⌊_⌋_⌊_⌋_⌋ ⌊_⌋_⌊_⌋ they can pay it on time. They are always ⌊_⌋_⌊_⌋_⌋_⌊_⌋_⌊_⌋_⌋ money from home. Of course, they ⌊_⌋_⌊_⌋_⌋_⌊_⌋_⌋_⌊_⌋ their parents' kindness. But they also work ⌊_⌋_⌊_⌋ ⌊_⌋_⌊_⌋_⌋ two hours a day.

PART B SOME WORDS BELOW ARE BOLD FACE. SUBSTITUTE THE ABOVE IDIOMS WHICH MEAN THE SAME THING. THEN COPY THE COMPLETE SENTENCE IN THE SAME TENSE AND PERSON.

1 I **anticipate with pleasure** your calling on me. _____

2 **As is her custom**, Betty finished her shopping early. _____
_____

3 **Check** that the door is locked. _____

4 Joe is **not less than** six feet tall. _____

5 We **profit greatly from** our language lab. _____

PART C WRITE THE APPROPRIATE IDIOM. MAKE IT AGREE IN TENSE AND PERSON WITH THE REST OF THE SENTENCE.

Sally saves her money. _____ , she paid her bills on time yesterday. By saving her money, she_____ she could always pay them. All last week she was wondering if her boyfriend remembered her; she was _____ a letter from him. Last Christmas she _____ her extra money to buy gifts for him. She also wrote him _____ twice a week.

PART D FILL IN THE BLANKS, USING ALL FIVE IDIOMS PLUS ONE FROM EXERCISE 14.

Frank always _____ his time and works hard _____ ten hours a day, sometimes more. Of course, he is always _____ to weekends when he can _____his alarm clock and sleep late.

Yesterday, _____, Frank awoke at five A.M. Because he didn't want to forget it, he_____ to wind his alarm clock right away. Then he found out it was Sunday.

PART E SUBSTITUTE THE CORRECT IDIOMS FOR THE BOLD FACE WORDS. THEN COPY THE WHOLE SENTENCE AND FINISH IT IN YOUR OWN WORDS.

1 I **checked** that he . . . . _____

2 **As is its custom**, the newspaper. . . . _____

3 We will **be anticipating with pleasure** . . . . _____

4 Frank was **not less than** 99 percent sure that Edward . . . ._____

_____

5 We will **profit greatly from** our vacation in England by . . . . _____

_____

PART F WRITE A PARAGRAPH ABOUT YOUR VACATION LAST SUMMER. USE ALL FIVE IDIOMS.

COLORFUL IDIOM: **GO DOWNHILL**. Lose your success or health.

test 5

A. DIRECTIONS

a   Rearrange the letters in each box to make an idiom and write it in the box.

b   Find the definition below that fits each idiom and put its *number* in the circle.

c   Add the numbers in the circles across (→) or down (↓). The numbers must total 34.

DEFINITIONS

1 not less than
2 start the operation of
3 as is or was the custom
4 continually
5 firstly, to begin with
6 anticipate with pleasure
7 stop the operation of
8 return from
9 to the extent that
10 insist upon
11 tolerate
12 profit greatly from
13 be certain, check
14 stay informed of
15 invite
16 have the habit of

SA ARF SA ○ ___	NI HET STRIF CLAPE ○ ___	DEUS OT ○ ___	LAL EHT MITE ○ ___ =34
TEG CABK ○ ___	KEAM A TINPO FO ○ ___	PEEK PU THIW ○ ___	RUNT NO ○ ___ =34
TUP UP HIWT ○ ___	NURT FOF ○ ___	SA ULUAS ○ ___	EKAM RESU ○ ___ =34
OKOL DRAWROF OT ○ ___	AKEM HET STOM FO ○ ___	TA STEAL ○ ___	AHEV VERO ○ ___ =34
=34	=34	=34	=34

MY NAME _____   TEACHER'S NAME _____   DATE _____

B FILL IN THE APPROPRIATE IDIOMS. USE EACH IDIOM ONLY ONCE, CHOOSING THE CORRECT TENSE AND PRONOUN.

make sure / turn off / at least / get back / make a point of / in the first place

1 Before we take a trip, I need _____ a week for the preparations.

2 _____, I buy two or three maps and find the most direct roads.

3 Next, I _____ finding out where the best restaurants are.

4 I let my husband _____ the car is in good condition.

5 We usually _____ the last day of our vacation.

C FROM PART E OF EXERCISES 13, 14, 15 YOUR INSTRUCTOR WILL READ ALOUD FIVE INCOMPLETE SENTENCES. COPY THEM DOWN. THEN DO AS YOU HAVE DONE BEFORE WITH PART E. SUBSTITUTE THE IDIOMS FROM THE LIST BELOW AND FINISH THE SENTENCES IN YOUR OWN WORDS. USE AN IDIOM ONLY ONCE.

as far as / used to / all the time / keep up with / turn on / put up with / as usual / look forward to / make the most of

1 _____

2 _____

3 _____

4 _____

5 _____

PROVERBS AND SAYINGS: THERE IS NONE SO DEAF AS HE WHO WILL NOT HEAR.

Part 2

PAST AND PERFECT TENSES (SIMPLE AND PROGRESSIVE)

exercise 16
American Last Names:
What They Tell Us

by far
figure out [S]
keep on
leave out [S]
look into

MIMI: Why are millions of Americans named Smith or Jones? I can't **figure** it **out.**

SAM: Don't omit the Browns, Johnsons and Williamses. You mustn't **leave** them **out**; there are millions of them, too.

MIMI: Aren't their names English?

SAM: Yes. At first, Americans who came from England were **by far** the largest group here. In 1790 they amounted to sixty-nine percent of the population.

MIMI: What about the other last names I **keep on** hearing all the time?

SAM: Well, between 1840 and 1855 a million and a half Irish entered the U.S. Consult any Chicago, New York or Boston phonebook and you'll find pages of O'Briens, Kennedys and Fitzgeralds. Then, after the Revolution of 1848 in Europe, millions of Germans came here. Americans owe their beer to Schlitz, Pabst, Budweiser, Schaeffer and other German immigrants.

MIMI: I'm thirsty. We can **look into** the subject later.

PART A   USING ALL FIVE IDIOMS, FILL IN THE BLANKS, ONE LETTER FOR EACH BLANK. MAKE EACH IDIOM AGREE IN TENSE AND PERSON WITH ITS SENTENCE.

Why has Tony Marco been ╱_╱_╱_╱_╱_╱ the best house builder in Detroit? Because year after year he ╱_╱_╱_╱_╱_╱_╱ building excellent houses at a reasonable price. How has he done this? First, because he ╱_╱_╱_╱_╱_╱_╱_╱_╱ exactly what he needs for the material of each house and never ╱_╱_╱_╱_╱_╱_╱_╱ a single brick or piece of wood. Second, because he carefully ╱_╱_╱_╱_╱_╱_╱_╱ the prices of material and chooses the best material at the lowest price.

PART B   SOME WORDS BELOW ARE BOLD FACE. SUBSTITUTE THE ABOVE IDIOMS WHICH MEAN THE SAME THING. THEN COPY THE COMPLETE SENTENCE IN THE SAME TENSE AND PERSON.

1 The bad boy **continued** throwing mud at me. _____

2 Have you **examined** various ways of earning money? _____

_____

3 Did you **omit** Stephen's name from the list? _____

4 Killy is **by the largest margin** France's greatest skier. _____

5 We can't **understand** what our boss wants us to do. _____

_____

MY NAME _____ TEACHER'S NAME_____ DATE_____

50

PART C WRITE THE APPROPRIATE IDIOM. MAKE IT AGREE IN TENSE AND PERSON WITH THE REST OF THE SENTENCE.

Having written fifty best-selling books, Betty Jones was _____ the most successful writer of the 1970's. How did she do it? In the first place, she always _____ trying to do her best. She also made a point of _____ the hidden taste of people and of _____ exactly how to give them what they liked. In fact, she seldom _____ of her books what people liked.

PART D FILL IN THE BLANKS, USING ALL FIVE IDIOMS PLUS ONE FROM EXERCISE 15.

I became curious about Don. I _____ his past life and discovered that he was a thief. He stole much more than other thieves. In fact, he was _____ the world's best thief; he stole _____ $1,000,000 a year. Year after year, he _____ stealing. The police never caught him. He always thought carefully and _____ ahead of time how to escape them. One day Don told me everything. He _____ nothing about his crimes.

PART E SUBSTITUTE THE CORRECT IDIOMS FOR THE BOLD FACE WORDS. THEN COPY THE WHOLE SENTENCE AND FINISH IT IN YOUR OWN WORDS.

1 In your letter to me, why have you **omitted** that. . . ? _____
_____

2 Gilbert is **examining** the possibility of. . . . _____

3 I have been **by the largest margin** the school's. . . . _____
_____

4 Our boss **continued** asking us to. . . . _____

5 Mimi hasn't **understood** why Sam. . . . _____

PART F WRITE ONE PARAGRAPH ABOUT TRYING TO FIND THE NAME OR ADDRESS OF SOMEONE. USE ALL FIVE IDIOMS.

COLORFUL IDIOM: **SHOOT OFF YOUR MOUTH.** Speak without restraint; talk too much.

exercise 17
A Land of Immigrants: Some Facts and Figures

by the way
let . . . see
look at
take part in
that is

MIMI: There are nearly as many Italians in New York City as in Venice. My teacher told me this.

SAM: And **look at** how many Jews live there. They could increase the population of Israel by two-thirds.

MIMI: When did they come to the U. S.?

SAM: The Italians and the Jews? Between 1880 and 1920 three million Jews, mostly from Eastern Europe, came here. Four and a half million Italians came, too. Oh, **by the way**, Frank Sinatra's mother and fatl were among those Italian immigrants.

MIMI: Who were the famous immigrants—**that is**, who were those who became famous American citizens?

SAM: **Let me see**. Sikorsky, inventor of the helicopter; Stravinsky, composer of modern music; and Heifetz, the great violinist, came from Russia. Mann, the novelist, and Einstein, the physicist, came from Germany. And from Italy—

MIMI: I'm always amazed at how many great men **have taken part in** American life.

PART A   USING ALL FIVE IDIOMS, FILL IN THE BLANKS, ONE LETTER FOR EACH BLANK. MAKE EACH IDIOM AGREE IN TENSE AND PERSON WITH ITS SENTENCE.

JACK: Do you want to | | | | | | | | | | | | | | a women's liberation meeting?

BOB: | | | | | | | | | | |. I have to | | | | | | | | my appointment book before I answer.

JACK: | | | | | | | | | |, your girlfriend will be one of the speakers.

BOB: You mean, I can join politics and love, | | | | | | | |, go to the meeting as well as see my girlfriend.

PART B   SOME WORDS BELOW ARE BOLD FACE. SUBSTITUTE THE ABOVE IDIOMS WHICH MEAN THE SAME THING. THEN COPY THE COMPLETE SENTENCE IN THE SAME TENSE AND PERSON.

1 When I **regarded** the tires of my car, I found nails in them. _____

_____

2 How many men **participated** in World War II? _____

3 **Allow me to think**. Where's the key? _____

4 I enjoyed the party; **incidentally**, I met Fred there. _____

_____

5 He's a big man—**to say it more exactly**, he's more than six feet tall. _____

_____

PART C WRITE THE APPROPRIATE IDIOM. MAKE IT AGREE IN TENSE AND PERSON WITH THE REST OF THE SENTENCE.

SAM: Did France _____ the Olympic games last summer?

MIMI: _____. I think it did. I'll have to _____ some old newspapers to be sure.

SAM: _____, my brother once belonged to Japan's Olympic swimming team.

MIMI: Your brother must be an excellent swimmer, _____, one of the best swimmers in the world.

PART D FILL IN THE BLANKS, USING ALL FIVE IDIOMS PLUS ONE FROM EXERCISE 16.

MIMI: Should I go shopping today? _____. I have to _____ what's in the refrigerator.

PATRICIA: Oh, _____, Mimi, there's a dress sale at Hillwood Plaza today. We can buy nice cheap, dresses _____, at half price.

MIMI: I love to _____ sales. I usually _____ searching until I find the dress I need. Yes, let's go.

PART E SUBSTITUTE THE CORRECT IDIOMS FOR THE BOLD FACE WORDS. THEN COPY THE WHOLE SENTENCE AND FINISH IT IN YOUR OWN WORDS.

1 (John has worked hard on his English.) **Incidentally**, he has. . . . _____

_____

2 Was Mildred a tall girl—**to say it more exactly**, was she. . .? _____

_____

3 **Allow us to think**. Where is. . .? _____

4 (Andrew loves sports.) He has **participated in**. . . . _____

_____

5 Jerry **regarded** the phonebook, hoping to find. . . . _____

_____

PART F WRITE ONE PARAGRAPH ABOUT SOMEONE WHO BECAME FAMOUS. USE ALL FIVE IDIOMS.

COLORFUL IDIOM: **SHARP AS A TACK.** Said of somebody clever, especially in practical affairs.

exercise 18
The American Woman Goes Shopping

all of a sudden
go up
more and more
take up [S]
up to

SAM: Yesterday my teacher asked me an interesting question: Why do American women buy more groceries than they need?

MIMI: **Up to** now I've only suspected American women were stupid. Now I know it.

SAM: A scientist hid movie cameras in a supermarket. He filmed the eyes of women buying groceries. When these women saw all the good things to eat, their eyes blinked **more and more** slowly. They seemed almost hypnotized. But when they came near the cash register, their blinking increased. It **went up** as much as one hundred percent, and they started to look worried.

MIMI: No wonder. **All of a sudden** they remembered they couldn't pay for everything they took.

SAM: How did you know?

MIMI: Recently the same thing happened to me. Maybe I should **take up** mathematics.

PART A   USING ALL FIVE IDIOMS, FILL IN THE BLANKS, ONE LETTER FOR EACH BLANK. MAKE EACH IDIOM AGREE IN TENSE AND PERSON WITH ITS SENTENCE.

In Europe and Asia many young people have / / / / / / / / / English. / / / / / / / now they hadn't known how interesting it could be. / / / / / / / / / / / / / / / / they have found out they like English. And as they study it / / / / / / / / / / / / / / / / / / /, it has become easier and easier. Unfortunately for them, the price of language books / / / / / / / / / each year.

PART B   SOME WORDS BELOW ARE BOLD FACE. SUBSTITUTE THE ABOVE IDIOMS WHICH MEAN THE SAME THING. THEN COPY THE COMPLETE SENTENCE IN THE SAME TENSE AND PERSON.

1 **Until** February he did well in chemistry. _____

2 **Without warning** the ceiling fell on my head. _____

3 I'm becoming **increasingly** interested in sports. _____

4 I've **begun** plumbing as a trade. _____

5 Meat prices **increase** every week. _____

PART C WRITE THE APPROPRIATE IDIOM. MAKE IT AGREE IN TENSE AND PERSON WITH THE REST OF THE SENTENCE.

In my high school many boys _____ tennis last year. _____ then they hadn't guessed how difficult tennis could be. _____ they discovered that hitting a ball was difficult. But as they played _____ , they became better and better. Unhappily for them, the cost of tennis balls _____ last summer.

PART D FILL IN THE BLANKS, USING ALL FIVE IDIOMS PLUS ONE FROM EXERCISE 17.

_____ there were no more lights in our house. A few minutes later we noticed that all of our neighbors had no lights, either. _____ then, we had thought my father had turned off the electricity to save money. He was always saying that the price of electricity was _____ too fast. Each price increase made him _____ angry. One day he seriously suggested that I _____ electricity so that I could work for the electric company. "Open your eyes," he told me, "and _____ all the money you'll make."

PART E SUBSTITUTE THE CORRECT IDIOMS FOR THE BOLD FACE WORDS. THEN COPY THE WHOLE SENTENCE AND FINISH IT IN YOUR OWN WORDS.

1 **Until** this year my life has been. . . . _____

2 Did Phil. . .**without warning**? _____

3 Every day that we don't study hard makes it **increasingly** difficult to. . . . _____
_____

4 I'm **beginning** photography as a way of. . . . _____

5 If the cost of living **increases**, we'll. . . . _____

PART F WRITE ONE PARAGRAPH ABOUT GOING SHOPPING. USE ALL FIVE IDIOMS.

COLORFUL IDIOM: **SHED CROCODILE TEARS.** Weep insincerely or show your grief hypocritically (from an old belief that crocodiles shed tears while eating their prey).

test 6

A. DIRECTIONS

a Rearrange the letters in each box to make an idiom and write it in the box.

b Find the definition below that fits each idiom and put its *number* in the circle.

c Add the numbers in the circles across (——▶) or down (▼). The numbers must total 34.

DEFINITIONS

1 anticipate with pleasure
2 regard, direct your eyes toward
3 increasingly
4 understand
5 omit
6 rise, increase
7 to say it more exactly
8 participate
9 by a great margin
10 continue
11 allow me to think
12 until
13 undertake, begin
14 incidentally
15 suddenly
16 investigate, examine

AVELE UTO ◯ ___	YB ARF ◯ ___	UREGIF UTO ◯ ___	OKLO TINO ◯ ___	=34
EPEK NO ◯ ___	KEAT TRAP NI ◯ ___	KOLO TA ◯ ___	YB TEH YAW ◯ ___	=34
ATTH SI ◯ ___	TEL EM ESE ◯ ___	KATE PU ◯ ___	ROME DAN ROME ◯ ___	=34
PU OT ◯ ___	OG PU ◯ ___	LAL FO A DENDUS ◯ ___	KOLO DRAWFOR OT ◯ ___	=34
=34	=34	=34	=34	

MY NAME _____ DATE _____

TEACHER'S NAME _____

55

B FILL IN THE APPROPRIATE IDIOMS. USE EACH IDIOM ONLY ONCE, CHOOSING THE CORRECT TENSE AND PRONOUN.

that is / by the way / more and more / **keep on** / all of a sudden / up to

1 "My math teacher gives me _____ homework," Joanna said.

2 "_____ last January I was the best student in her class."

3 "But _____ I became sick. It happened very quickly."

4 "_____, my math teacher became sick, too." Did you know that?

5 "I feel better now, but if I _____ working so hard I'll become sick again."

C FROM PART E OF EXERCISES 16, 17, 18 YOUR INSTRUCTOR WILL READ ALOUD FIVE INCOMPLETE SENTENCES. COPY THEM DOWN. THEN DO AS YOU HAVE DONE BEFORE WITH PART E: SUBSTITUTE THE IDIOMS FROM THE LIST BELOW AND FINISH THE SENTENCES IN YOUR OWN WORDS. USE AN IDIOM ONLY ONCE.

leave out / by far / figure out / look into / make up / look at / let. . .see / go up / take up

1 _____

2 _____

3 _____

4 _____

5 _____

PROVERBS AND SAYINGS: **PEOPLE WHO LIVE IN GLASS HOUSES SHOULDN'T THROW STONES.**

exercise 19
Modern United States Houses: Every One Alike

it is a question of
let . . . alone
no matter
not much of a
tell A from B

MIMI: Modern American houses all look the same.
SAM: You must be colorblind! Can't you **tell** brown houses **from** green ones?
MIMI: Do you think **it's a question of** color? Americans build their houses the same **no matter** what color they paint them.
SAM: I'm only joking.
MIMI: Can't you stop joking? Can't you **let** me **alone**?
SAM: I'm sorry!
MIMI: As I was saying, in American towns half the houses are ranch houses. Now—
SAM: A *ranch* house—what's that?
MIMI: It's a one-story house, long, with **not much of a** roof. A very low roof, in fact. Like most American houses, it's made of wood.

PART A   USING ALL FIVE IDIOMS, FILL IN THE BLANKS, ONE LETTER FOR EACH BLANK. MAKE EACH IDIOM AGREE IN TENSE AND PERSON WITH ITS SENTENCE.

Herbert has to live in one room and wear old clothes. ⌐/⌐/⌐/⌐/⌐/⌐/⌐/⌐/⌐/⌐/⌐/⌐/⌐/⌐/⌐/ ⌐/⌐/ money. ⌐/⌐/⌐/⌐/⌐/⌐/⌐/ how hard he works, he never has enough money. His room is small and dirty. It's ⌐/⌐/⌐/⌐/⌐/⌐/⌐/⌐/⌐/⌐/ room to live in. He has no calendar on the wall and he can't ⌐/⌐/⌐/⌐/ one day ⌐/⌐/⌐/⌐/ the next. Even when he has almost no money, his friends don't ⌐/⌐/⌐/⌐/⌐/⌐/⌐/⌐/⌐/⌐/. They keep on trying to borrow from him.

PART B   SOME WORDS BELOW ARE BOLD FACE. SUBSTITUTE THE ABOVE IDIOMS WHICH MEAN THE SAME THING. THEN COPY THE COMPLETE SENTENCE IN THE SAME TENSE AND PERSON.

1 No wine, no girls: it was **a rather bad** party. _____

2 We can't go to Europe this summer. It **doesn't concern** money; it **concerns** time. _____

_____

3 Can you **distinguish** real money **from** false? _____

4 **Regardless of** how nice I was, he always found fault with me. _____

_____

5 "**Allow** me **to be undisturbed**," I said. _____

MY NAME_____ TEACHER'S NAME _____ DATE _____

PART C   WRITE THE APPROPRIATE IDIOM. MAKE IT AGREE IN TENSE AND PERSON WITH THE REST OF THE SENTENCE.

Joan had to go to the hospital yesterday. _____ life or death. _____ what medicine she used, she was never healthy. The hospital was noisy and crowded. It was _____ hospital to go to. She had so many pains she couldn't _____ one pain _____ another. Even when she felt better, her doctors didn't _____ They kept on giving her new medicine.

PART D   FILL IN THE BLANKS, USING ALL FIVE IDIOMS PLUS ONE FROM EXERCISE 18.

When my father was young, ordinary people didn't cheat or steal. For these people _____ honesty. _____ how poor they were, they were never dishonest. If a man was a thief, people avoided him and _____ .

Today people _____ stealing as a hobby. For them, stealing a few dollars is _____ crime because they can no longer _____ right _____ wrong.

PART E   SUBSTITUTE THE CORRECT IDIOMS FOR THE BOLD FACE WORDS. THEN COPY THE WHOLE SENTENCE AND FINISH IT IN YOUR OWN WORDS.

1 If you can't **distinguish** left **from** right, you'll never become. . . . _____

_____

2 The children must **allow** the dog **to be undisturbed** or it will. . . . _____

_____

3 **Regardless of** who may disagree, Sam has been _____

_____

4 Joe couldn't come; it **concerned** not having. . . . _____

_____

5 It has been **a rather bad** vacation for me because. . . . _____

_____

PART F   WRITE ONE PARAGRAPH ABOUT YOUR IDEA OF A NICE HOUSE. USE ALL FIVE IDIOMS.

COLORFUL IDIOM: **SNUG AS A BUG IN A RUG.** To be warm, comfortable and secure.

exercise 20
Sam and Mimi
Become Friends Again

about to
ask for [S]
might as well
outside of
take place

MIMI: I don't understand how you can like modern American art.

SAM: I love it! I went to every modern art show that **took place** in New York last year.

MIMI: Whose paintings do you like best?

SAM: Jackson Pollock's. **Outside of** three or four of his early ones, I admire everything he did. By the way, did you know that the Guggenheim Museum is showing his work this week? You might want to go.

MIMI: **Are** you **asking** me **for** a date?

SAM: Yes, I was **about to** ask you. But perhaps you're still angry with me?

MIMI: Not at all. But after last week, I didn't think you wanted to see me again.

SAM: I **might as well** admit that at first I didn't. But now I think both of us were silly.

MIMI: Speak for yourself, Sam!

PART A   USING ALL FIVE IDIOMS, FILL IN THE BLANKS, ONE LETTER FOR EACH BLANK. MAKE EACH IDIOM AGREE IN TENSE AND PERSON WITH ITS SENTENCE.

On the highways of America, accidents /_/_/_/_/_/_/_/_/_/ every minute. At this very moment an accident is /_/_/_/_/_/_/_/ happen. /_/_/_/_/_/_/_/_/_/_/ a small number, however, who drive too fast, most Americans drive within the speed limit. But those who don't obey the law /_/_/_/_/_/_/_/_/_/_/_/ be trying to kill themselves and everybody else. That is why many Americans /_/_/_/_/_/_/_/_/_/_/_/_/ stronger laws against fast drivers.

PART B   SOME WORDS BELOW ARE BOLD FACE. SUBSTITUTE THE ABOVE IDIOMS WHICH MEAN THE SAME THING. THEN COPY THE COMPLETE SENTENCE IN THE SAME TENSE AND PERSON.

1 My wife has **requested** a divorce. _____

2 Mimi was **on the point of** cry(ing) when Sam telephoned. _____

3 **Except for** Jim, the teacher likes all the students._____

4 Where has the murder **happened**? _____

5 I **could with equal or better effect** lie; nobody believes me anyway. _____

_____

MY NAME _____   TEACHER'S NAME _____   DATE _____

PART C   WRITE THE APPROPRIATE IDIOM. MAKE IT AGREE IN TENSE AND PERSON WITH THE REST OF THE SENTENCE.

Last year, in the churches of Boston, two hundred marriages _____ every week. Everywhere men and women were _____ get married. _____ a few who married after a long friendship, many married too quickly. Some girls even _____ a heaven on earth. Because they will never have it, they _____ have given up the idea ahead of time.

PART D   FILL IN THE BLANKS, USING ALL FIVE IDIOMS PLUS ONE FROM EXERCISE 19.

_____ Benjamin, I was the hardest worker in the company. So yesterday I ____,_____ a raise in salary. "If I don't get $20 more a week," I told my boss, "I _____ quit. It _____ justice." At five, when I was _____ stop work, he told me to come to his office. Obviously I wasn't ready for what _____ there. My boss fired me.

PART E   SUBSTITUTE THE CORRECT IDIOMS FOR THE BOLD FACE WORDS. THEN COPY THE WHOLE SENTENCE AND FINISH IT IN YOUR OWN WORDS.

1 When Frank arrived, were you **on the point of**...? _____
_____

2 Carol has **requested** a.... _____

3 **Except for** math, I've.... _____

4 Many crimes have **happened** since.... _____

5 Since Harry had nothing to do, he **could with equal or better effect** have.... _____
_____

PART F   WRITE A PARAGRAPH ABOUT AN ARGUMENT YOU HAD. USE ALL FIVE IDIOMS.

COLORFUL IDIOM: **WEAR YOUR HEART ON YOUR SLEEVE.** Show your sentiments and emotions openly

exercise 21
Mimi Asks About
the Race Problem

as long as
as yet
even so
once and for all
step by step

MIMI: Why does America have a race problem?
SAM: Because different races live here.
MIMI: Sam, **once and for all**, be serious.
SAM: But I am serious, Mimi. A country doesn't have race problems **as long as** its citizens belong to one race. In England, for example, race problems didn't exist until thousands of people from Africa and Asia came to live there. Then it had a large racial minority for the first time in its history and troubles started.
MIMI: But that doesn't excuse the U.S.
SAM: Of course not. But racism is an old problem. **As yet**, no nation has completely solved it.
MIMI: **Even so**, isn't the U.S. terribly racist?
SAM: How many countries do you know with a racial minority of 11 percent or more?
MIMI: South Africa? Maybe three or four others?
SAM: Unlike those countries, however, America has been moving **step by step** toward racial equality.

PART A   USING ALL FIVE IDIOMS, FILL IN THE BLANKS, ONE LETTER FOR EACH BLANK. MAKE EACH IDIOM AGREE IN TENSE AND PERSON WITH ITS SENTENCE.

When Jill baked, she always added or subtracted something. That was why she couldn't be sure, / / / / / / / / / / / / / / / / / /, her cakes and pies would succeed. What she needed was more practice, for / / / / / / / she was not a very skillful cook.

Today Jill has been practicing her baking. She has proceeded / / / / / / / / / / / / / to mix sugar, eggs, butter and flour. She knows that she will have no trouble / / / / / / / / / / she follows directions exactly. / / / / / / / /, the silly girl has decided to add extra butter and sugar.

PART B   SOME WORDS BELOW ARE BOLD FACE. SUBSTITUTE THE ABOVE IDIOMS WHICH MEAN THE SAME THING. THEN COPY THE COMPLETE SENTENCE IN THE SAME TENSE AND PERSON.

1 Has the world been progressing **by degrees** toward peace? _____

_____

2 **Until now**, my brother hasn't learned to play baseball well. _____

_____

MY NAME _____ TEACHER'S NAME _____ DATE _____

3 Bob wanted, **finally and forever**, to forget the past. _____

_____

4 **Provided that** you do your best tomorrow, no one will blame you._____

_____

5 Mr. Smith is a rich man, but **nevertheless** he shouldn't feel so proud. _____

_____

PART C   WRITE THE APPROPRIATE IDIOM. MAKE IT AGREE IN TENSE AND PERSON WITH THE REST OF THE SENTENCE.

_____ John studied hard, he did well in English. Miss Jones, his teacher, helped him, too. She carefully and slowly taught him all the verbs. _____ he learned their present, their past and their future tenses.

John was Miss Jones' best student. _____, he made many mistakes in English, and he often became discouraged.

"Cheer up," she told him. "For years men have looked for a quick way to learn a foreign language. _____ , they haven't found it. So you must learn, _____ , that there is no easy road to success."

PART D   FILL IN THE BLANKS, USING ALL FIVE IDIOMS PLUS ONE FROM EXERCISE 20.

Larry was _____take a trip when he had a heart attack. No wonder that after he left the hospital, he decided, _____, to exercise regularly. He had found out that _____ he walked a lot, he felt wonderful. _____, he knew enough not to walk too much.

The doctors say that Larry is advancing _____ toward good health. _____, he is not completely healthy, but he soon will be.

PART E   SUBSTITUTE THE CORRECT IDIOMS FOR THE BOLD FACE WORDS. THEN COPY THE WHOLE SENTENCE AND FINISH IT IN YOUR OWN WORDS.

1 (My father had expected me home early.) **Nevertheless** I. . . . _____

_____

2 **Provided that** he worked hard, Tim felt. . . . _____

3 Have you decided, **finally and forever**, to. . . . _____

_____

4 **Until now**, there has been no evidence for. . . ._____

_____

5 Rita has been learning **by degrees** to. . . . _____

PART F   WRITE ONE PARAGRAPH ABOUT RACIAL PROBLEMS IN THE U.S. USE ALL FIVE IDIOMS.

COLORFUL IDIOM: **WEAR YOUR BIRTHDAY SUIT.** Be absolutely naked.

test 7

A. DIRECTIONS

a Rearrange the letters in each box to make an idiom and write it in the box.

b Find the definition below that fits each idiom and put its *number* in the circle.

c Add the numbers in the circles across (—→) or down (↓). The numbers must total 34.

DEFINITIONS

1 provided that
2 it concerns
3 participate
4 allow somebody to be undisturbed
5 happen, occur
6 gradually
7 finally, decisively
8 rather bad
9 ready to, on the point of
10 regardless of
11 up to the present time
12 could with equal or better effect
13 nevertheless
14 distinguish between
15 except for
16 request something

TI SI A STUQIONE OF ◯ ____	ON TAMTRE ◯ ____	TON CHUM FO A ◯ ____	LELT A MORF B ◯ ____	=34
TEL ANEOL ◯ ____	AKET CLEAP ◯ ____	BUTOA OT ◯ ____	KAS FRO ◯ ____	=34
TIDESUO FO ◯ ____	THIMG SA LEWL ◯ ____	PETS YB PETS ◯ ____	SA GONL SA ◯ ____	=34
VENE OS ◯ ____	CONE DAN ROF LAL ◯ ____	SA ETY ◯ ____	TEKA TARP NI ◯ ____	=34
=34	=34	=34	=34	

MY NAME _____ TEACHER'S NAME _____ DATE _____

B   FILL IN THE APPROPRIATE IDIOMS. USE EACH IDIOM ONLY ONCE, CHOOSING THE CORRECT TENSE AND PRONOUN.

not much of a / no matter / even so / ask for / about to / as long as

1 *Fanny:* "Oh, Hello Sam! I was _____ call you."

2 I wanted to _____ your help.

3 _____ how hard I try to do my math, I don't understand it.

4 I guess I'm _____ mathematician!"

5 *Sam:* "I'll try to help you. _____, you'll have to do a lot of work yourself."

C   FROM PART E OF EXERCISES 19, 20, 21 YOUR INSTRUCTOR WILL READ ALOUD FIVE INCOMPLETE SENTENCES. COPY THEM DOWN. THEN DO AS YOU HAVE DONE BEFORE WITH PART E: SUBSTITUTE THE IDIOMS FROM THE LIST BELOW AND FINISH THE SENTENCES IN YOUR OWN WORDS. USE AN IDIOM ONLY ONCE.

It is a question of / tell A from B / let. . .alone / take place / outside of / might as well / step by step / once and for all / as yet

1 _____

2 _____

3 _____

4 _____

5 _____

PROVERBS AND SAYINGS: **BETTER LATE THAN NEVER.**

exercise 22
Sam Doesn't Phone

all along
call up [S]
go away
make fun of
on purpose

MIMI: Why didn't you **call** me **up**? You promised you would.
SAM: I had to **go away** on business. Each time I called up, your phone was busy. I tried four times.
MIMI: I thought you didn't phone **on purpose**. . .that you didn't want to talk to me.
SAM: Suspicious little girl!
MIMI: Don't **make fun of** me. I even cried a little this afternoon.
SAM: Really? Forgive me.
MIMI: You knew **all along** that I liked you. But how do you feel about me?
SAM: I think you're. . .wonderful!

PART A   USING ALL FIVE IDIOMS, FILL IN THE BLANKS, ONE LETTER FOR EACH BLANK. MAKE EACH IDIOM AGREE IN TENSE AND PERSON WITH ITS SENTENCE.

The day Peter / / / / / / / / / on a trip to Miami, Hazel cried and cried. Of course, he / / / / / / / / / / / / the minute he arrived there and told her he loved her. She was pleased to hear it even though she had known it / / / / / / / / / /. She had known, too, that he wouldn't make her cry / / / / / / / / / / /. Even so, she tried to make him feel guilty for leaving her. But Peter only laughed. In fact, he / / / / / / / / / / / her.

PART B   SOME WORDS BELOW ARE BOLD FACE. SUBSTITUTE THE ABOVE IDIOMS WHICH MEAN THE SAME THING. THEN COPY THE COMPLETE SENTENCE IN THE SAME TENSE AND PERSON.

1 They had intended **from the beginning** to take us with them. _____

_____

2 She **telephoned** her boss at 7 A.M. _____

3 Her husband had **left** and never returned. _____

4 So she did it **for a reason**? _____

5 Please don't **laugh at me**; I don't like it. _____

MY NAME _____ TEACHER'S NAME _____ DATE _____

PART C   WRITE THE APPROPRIATE IDIOM. MAKE IT AGREE IN TENSE AND PERSON WITH THE REST OF THE SENTENCE.

Last week Dave's ex-girlfriend _____ and told him she hated him. He had been hoping _____ that she would forget his phone number. He was even glad when she _____ to another city. Of course, he knew that she was trying to make him sad _____ . In the past, whenever he had tried to be nice to her, she _____ him and laughed at him.

PART D   FILL IN THE BLANKS, USING ALL FIVE IDIOMS PLUS ONE FROM EXERCISE 21.

Last year my brother _____ . He moved to California. _____ he stayed there, he didn't write his girlfriend and he didn't _____ . Why? Because she had always _____ him and he hadn't liked it. So he had ignored her _____ .

But my brother must have felt _____ that she loved him. He married her when he got back from California.

PART E   SUBSTITUTE THE CORRECT IDIOMS FOR THE BOLD FACE WORDS. THEN COPY THE WHOLE SENTENCE AND FINISH IT IN YOUR OWN WORDS.

1 I. . .**for a reason**. _____

2 Sam had **laughed at** Mimi because. . . . _____

3 Dave had **left** before. . . . _____

4 If I had **telephoned** my parents earlier, they. . . . _____

_____

5 My teacher had known **from the beginning** that. . . . _____

_____

PART F   WRITE ONE PARAGRAPH ABOUT A TELEPHONE CONVERSATION YOU RECENTLY HAD. USE ALL FIVE IDIOMS.

COLORFUL IDIOM: **CRY YOUR EYES OUT.** Weep much and bitterly.

exercise 23
Religion in America:
Some Facts

call off [S]
have in mind [S]
keep quiet [S]
look up [S]
read up on

SAM: All day long **I've been reading up on** religion in America.
MIMI: **I've looked up** quite a few facts myself. Did you know that the U.S. has twice as many Jews—
SAM: As Israel.
MIMI: That it has as many Catholics—
SAM: As France.
MIMI: As for Protestants—
SAM: There are 72,000,000 of them and they belong to over 200 denominations.
MIMI: Besides the Bu. . .
SAM: Buddhists, Moslems and Hindus, there are about 4,000,000 Orthodox Christians.
MIMI: You win! **I'm calling off** the contest.
SAM: But I'm not finished. **Keep quiet** and listen. Did you know that only two religions are native to the United States—Christian Science and Mormonism? Did you know—
MIMI: No, I didn't know you **had in mind** becoming my teacher when you asked me for a date. I feel like I'm at school.

PART A USING ALL FIVE IDIOMS, FILL IN THE BLANKS, ONE LETTER FOR EACH BLANK. MAKE EACH IDIOM AGREE IN TENSE AND PERSON.

William had been a good history student. He had listened carefully to his teacher, |_|_|_|_|_| |_|_|_|_|_|_| in class, and written many notes. In the month before his final exam, he |_|_|_|_| |_|_|_|_|_|_|_|_|_| two hundred years of United States history and |_|_|_|_|_|_| |_|_| the names of all the states and their capitals. He obviously |_|_|_|_| |_|_|_|_| |_|_|_|_|_| being first in his class, for he |_|_|_|_| even |_|_|_|_|_|_|_|_|_|_| his dates with his girlfriend and had studied every night.

PART B SOME WORDS BELOW ARE BOLD FACE. SUBSTITUTE THE ABOVE IDIOMS WHICH MEAN THE SAME THING. THEN COPY THE COMPLETE SENTENCE IN THE SAME TENSE AND PERSON.

1 Has the salesman **searched for** the prices on his list? _____

_____

2 For a long time I have **planned** a trip to St. Louis. _____

_____

MY NAME _____ TEACHER'S NAME _____ DATE _____

3 We had **remained silent** until she asked our opinion. _____

_____

4 My father **cancelled** the trip because I was sick. _____

_____

5 I had **studied by reading** about the art of Picasso before I went to the museum. _____

_____

PART C   WRITE THE APPROPRIATE IDIOM. MAKE IT AGREE IN TENSE AND PERSON WITH THE REST OF THE SENTENCE.

After he failed his history test, Joe learned that he _____ the wrong war and that he _____ the wrong dates. But it was his own fault: If he _____ in class and had listened to his teacher, he would have passed the test. Instead, he had thought very little about history, for he _____ impressing the pretty girl sitting beside him. He _____ even _____ an appointment with his history teacher to meet this girl downtown.

PART D   FILL IN THE BLANKS, USING ALL FIVE IDIOMS PLUS ONE FROM EXERCISE 22.

Last Saturday my father _____ our fishing trip and told me I had to stay at home. He said he wanted to speak to me. While he was speaking, I _____ and didn't say anything. I had been wanting _____ to find out what he planned to do. I was really curious about what he _____ for me.

What bad luck! Friday he had asked the secretary at my school to _____ my grades for him. Now I am spending my Saturdays _____ math and history.

PART E   SUBSTITUTE THE CORRECT IDIOMS FOR THE BOLD FACE WORDS. THEN COPY THE WHOLE SENTENCE AND FINISH IT IN YOUR OWN WORDS.

1 Mimi has **studied by reading** all the facts about. . . . _____

_____

2 The football coach had **cancelled** our game rather than. . . . _____

_____

3 My friends **remained silent** while. . . . _____

4 Before my wife suggested going shopping, I had **planned**. . . . _____

_____

5 Did Janet **search for** new words. . . ? _____

PART F   WRITE ONE PARAGRAPH ABOUT RELIGION IN YOUR COUNTRY. USE ALL FIVE IDIOMS.

COLORFUL IDIOM: **I DON'T HAVE A LEG TO STAND ON.** A person says this when he has no defense, excuse, or justification.

exercise 24

Americans: Are They a Social People?

every other
give back [S]
let go of
make out [S]
run out of

MIMI: Sam, **let go of** my hands! I want to point at something.

SAM: O.K., but I want a kiss for **giving** them **back** to you.

MIMI: Stop it! You're becoming too Americanized! Now answer me: What is similar about all those houses?

SAM: Is it that **every other** one has a two-car garage?

MIMI: No. Look at the land around them. What do you see?

SAM: Grass.

MIMI: What else?

SAM: I give up. I've **run out of** ideas.

MIMI: You're not trying. Can't you see that only one of those houses has a fence. In France our houses often have big, solid fences around them.

SAM: For years I've been trying to **make out** why the French are different from other people. Now I've figured it out: They don't trust one another.

PART A   USING ALL FIVE IDIOMS, FILL IN THE BLANKS, ONE LETTER FOR EACH BLANK. MAKE EACH IDIOM AGREE IN TENSE AND PERSON WITH ITS SENTENCE.

Sam and Mimi liked American films. / / / / / / / / / / / / / night they went to the movies. In the dark they held hands. Whenever he / / / / / / / / / her hand, she felt sad. By his smile, however, she / / / / / / / / / he wasn't angry at her.

But how could he be angry? He still owed her ten dollars. In fact, every time he / / / / / / / / / / / / money he borrowed a few dollars from her. Of course, he / / / / / it / / / / / to her in a week or two.

PART B   SOME WORDS BELOW ARE BOLD FACE. SUBSTITUTE THE ABOVE IDIOMS WHICH MEAN THE SAME THING. THEN COPY THE COMPLETE SENTENCE IN THE SAME TENSE AND PERSON.

1 Has Bruce **exhausted his supply of** cigarettes? _____

2 **Release** the handle; I can carry it. _____

3 Can you **understand** what he is saying? _____

4 **Return** me my pen. _____

5 The word "biennial" means occurring on **alternate years.** _____

MY NAME _____ TEACHER'S NAME _____ DATE _____

PART C   WRITE THE APPROPRIATE IDIOM. MAKE IT AGREE IN TENSE AND PERSON WITH THE REST OF THE SENTENCE.

Bob's dog would run away the moment he _____ of its rope. It seemed to him that it was running away _____ minute. Luckily it would always bark, and he was able to _____ where it had gone.

When the dog disappeared again yesterday, Bob finally_____patience. He _____ to the man who sold it to him.

PART D   FILL IN THE BLANKS, USING ALL FIVE IDIOMS PLUS ONE FROM EXERCISE 23.

Marge's beautiful dish broke on the floor when Herman accidentally _____ it. He had tried to excuse himself, but he soon _____ words. For the rest of the dinner he_____ .

The following day he bought another dish. Of course, he could not _____Marge _____ the same dish, but from what he could _____, the new one looked like the one he had dropped.

When Mary received it, she thanked him for it. Naturally she kept on inviting him to dinner _____ week.

PART E   SUBSTITUTE THE CORRECT IDIOMS FOR THE BOLD FACE WORDS. THEN COPY THE WHOLE SENTENCE AND FINISH IT IN YOUR OWN WORDS.

1 After his car had **exhausted its supply of** gas, he. . . . _____

_____

2 If your friend had **returned** the money to me, I. . . ._____

_____

3 The salesman stopped at **alternate** house(s) because. . . . _____

_____

4 Have you **understood** why. . . . _____

5 Sam **released** Mimi's hand while. . . ._____

PART F   WRITE ONE PARAGRAPH ABOUT "DATING" IN YOUR COUNTRY. USE ALL FIVE IDIOMS.

COLORFUL IDIOM: **BURN THE CANDLE AT BOTH ENDS.** Work or play too much so that your energy is quickly gone.

test 8

A. DIRECTIONS

a Rearrange the letters in each box to make an idiom and write it in the box.

b Find the definition below that fits each idiom and put its *number* in the circle.

c Add the numbers in the circles across (→) or down (↓). The numbers must total 34.

DEFINITIONS

1 alternate, every second one
2 understand
3 telephone
4 remain silent
5 study by reading about
6 return something
7 depart, leave
8 release
9 search for (in a book of reference)
10 cancel
11 from the beginning
12 exhaust your supply of
13 intentionally
14 intend, plan
15 allow somebody to be undisturbed
16 laugh at, ridicule

ALCL PU ◯ ___	OG AYAW ◯ ___	LAL GALON ◯ ___	NO RUPSPOE ◯ ___	=34
KEMA NUF FO ◯ ___	DEAR PU NO ◯ ___	LOKO PU ◯ ___	PEKE TIQUE ◯ ___	=34
EVAH NI DIMN ◯ ___	LCLA FOF ◯ ___	TEL OG FO ◯ ___	AKME UTO ◯ ___	=34
ERVEY ROTHE ◯ ___	NUR UOT FO ◯ ___	VIGE CABK ◯ ___	TEL LANEO ◯ ___	=34
=34	=34	=34	=34	

B FILL IN THE APPROPRIATE IDIOMS. USE EACH IDIOM ONLY ONCE, CHOOSING THE CORRECT TENSE AND PRONOUN.

look up / let go of / go away / on purpose / have in mind/ call up

1 Last Tuesday I _____ Mary from Washington.

2 I was _____ some facts at the Library of Congress there.

3 Mary asked why she hadn't received a phone call from me Monday. She thought I didn't phone _____ .

4 I told her that I _____ phoning her but that I forgot.

5 "The next time I _____ ," she said angrily, "I won't phone you, either."

C FROM PART E OF EXERCISES 22, 23, 24 YOUR INSTRUCTOR WILL READ ALOUD FIVE INCOMPLETE SENTENCES. COPY THEM DOWN. THEN DO AS YOU HAVE DONE BEFORE WITH PART E: SUBSTITUTE THE IDIOMS FROM THE LIST BELOW AND FINISH THE SENTENCES IN YOUR OWN WORDS. USE AN IDIOM ONLY ONCE.

all along / make fun of / keep quiet / call off / make out / every other / read up on / run out of / give back

1 _____

2 _____

3 _____

4 _____

5 _____

PROVERBS AND SAYINGS: **NEVER SAY DIE.**

exercise 25

A Sexy
Hairdo

for once
go out (to)
have (someone) do (something)
just now
look for

SAM: Where were you? I've **been looking for** you.
MIMI: I've **just now** got back. I've been shopping.
SAM: I've got two theater tickets. Want to **go out** tonight?
MIMI: I'd love to. But have you noticed my hair? I **had** Alphonse **do** the cut in a style you like.
SAM: It certainly makes you look . . . sexy.
MIMI: Look sexy? I am sexy. I'm a Frenchwoman.
SAM: **For once**, I agree with you.

PART A   USING ALL FIVE IDIOMS, FILL IN THE BLANKS, ONE LETTER FOR EACH BLANK. MAKE EACH IDIOM AGREE IN TENSE AND PERSON WITH ITS SENTENCE.

The best tailor in New Orleans was a friend of mine, so I /__/__/__/__/__/__/__/ my tailoring the way I like it and, /__/__/__/__/__/__/ , I got the suit I wanted. I didn't expect to hear today that my suit was ready, but /__/__/__/__/__/__/ he called up to tell me to come and get it. Although I was eager to put it on, I had to /__/__/__/__/__/__/ lunch with friends first and then /__/__/__/__/__/ some shirts to match my suit.

PART B   SOME WORDS BELOW ARE BOLD FACE. SUBSTITUTE THE ABOVE IDIOMS WHICH MEAN THE SAME THING. THEN COPY THE COMPLETE SENTENCE IN THE SAME TENSE AND PERSON.

1 Have you **made** your sister **do** your housework? _____

_____

2 Mimi **attended** lunch with Sam. _____

3 I met him in the hall **a moment ago**. _____

4 I've been **searching for** you everywhere! _____

5 **This one time**, did you do your homework? _____

PART C   WRITE THE APPROPRIATE IDIOM. MAKE IT AGREE IN TENSE AND PERSON WITH THE REST OF THE SENTENCE.

_____, my wife and I have bought the house we needed. The most honest builders in Detroit were friends of ours, and we have _____ the work. We had expected to hear yesterday that our house was finished and to come and visit it. But since they have _____ told us it isn't, we'll _____ shopping instead. Then my wife can _____curtains to hang in the house.

PART D   FILL IN THE BLANKS, USING ALL FIVE IDIOMS PLUS ONE FROM EXERCISE 24.

My brother is lazy; he is always _____ an easy way to do his homework. It seems as if _____ day he gets help from the other students. He_____ his homework for him.

But today, _____, he found no one to do it. Even so, he _____ to see a movie. He has _____ left the house.

PART E   SUBSTITUTE THE CORRECT IDIOMS FOR THE BOLD FACE WORDS. THEN COPY THE WHOLE SENTENCE AND FINISH IT IN YOUR OWN WORDS.

1 I have **made** the mechanic **do** the repairs on my car today so that. . . . _____

_____

2 Sam had thought that **attending** plays would be. . . . _____

_____

3 **A moment ago** I heard that. . . . _____
4 **This one time** , did Mimi . . . ? _____
5 He has been **searching for**. . . . _____

PART F   WRITE ONE PARAGRAPH ABOUT GOING TO A BARBER OR HAIRDRESSER. USE ALL FIVE IDIOMS.

COLORFUL IDIOM: **HAVE ONE FOOT IN THE GRAVE.** Be very ill, old, or infirm; be near death.

exercise 26
Are American Women Individualists?

have on [S]
instead of
just the same
once in a while
would rather

MIMI: I thought American women were conformists. Now I've discovered—at least as far as their clothes are concerned—it isn't so. Don't you agree?

SAM: I can't say. **Instead of** looking at their clothes, I look at other things.

MIMI: **Just the same**, you must have noticed the clothes those women wore last night. Some of them wore minis, some wore midis, and some wore maxis. Some even **had on** evening gowns, and a few came in short pants.

SAM: You're forgetting the women's liberation group.

MIMI: You mean those horrible girls without bras or girdles.

SAM: They only wanted to show themselves as they really were. Natural.

MIMI: **I would rather** be unnatural.

SAM: And beautiful!

MIMI: You say the nicest things. . .**once in a while.**

PART A USING ALL FIVE IDIOMS, FILL IN THE BLANKS, ONE LETTER FOR EACH BLANK. MAKE EACH IDIOM AGREE IN TENSE AND PERSON WITH ITS SENTENCE.

/ / / / / / / / / / / studying English, Pablo has been to the movies every night this week. But just now he is busy studying. / / / / / / / / / / / / / / / he feels like learning something. / / / / / / / / / / / /, English can never interest him as much as the movies do. He / / / / / / / / / / / / / go to the movies than study. When Pablo goes to the movies, he often / / / / / / / a blue suit and black shoes.

PART B SOME WORDS BELOW ARE BOLD FACE. SUBSTITUTE THE ABOVE IDIOMS WHICH MEAN THE SAME THING. THEN COPY THE COMPLETE SENTENCE IN THE SAME TENSE AND PERSON.

1 I'm usually polite; **nevertheless**, I can be impolite. _____

2 She often **wore** her blue sweater. _____

3 I've called on my grandmother **occasionally**. _____

4 I **prefer to** stay home tonight. _____

5 I'll be staying here **rather than** going there. _____

MY NAME _____ TEACHER'S NAME _____ DATE _____

PART C   WRITE THE APPROPRIATE IDIOM. MAKE IT AGREE IN TENSE AND PERSON WITH THE REST OF THE SENTENCE.

_____ going out on dates and having a good time , Maria and Estella studied English every night this week. But tonight they _____ pretty dresses and they're going out to a dance. _____ they feel like relaxing. _____ , dancing is never as important to them as English. They _____ do well in English than have a good time.

PART D   FILL IN THE BLANKS, USING ALL FIVE IDIOMS PLUS ONE FROM EXERCISE 25.

Occasionally I'm forgetful. _____ I can't remember where I've left my money and I have to _____ it. For example, last month I found it on the floor _____ in my pocket. Of course, I hadn't really lost it. _____ , I felt nervous. After that, I checked my pockets whenever I _____ a new suit. I _____ make sure than feel nervous, wouldn't you?

PART E   SUBSTITUTE THE CORRECT IDIOMS FOR THE BOLD FACE WORDS. THEN COPY THE WHOLE SENTENCE AND FINISH IT IN YOUR OWN WORDS.

1 To lose weight, Janet walks to work **rather than** . . . . _____

_____

2 If we have a choice, we **prefer** . . . . . _____

_____

3 Since yesterday I have **worn** my . . . . _____

_____

4 **Occasionally** Sam and Mimi . . . . _____
5 (Norman usually doesn't make any mistakes in English.) **Nevertheless**, he. . .yesterday._____

_____

PART F   WRITE ONE PARAGRAPH ABOUT HOW WELL (BADLY) SOME WOMEN DRESS. USE ALL FIVE IDIOMS.

COLORFUL IDIOM: **HAVE ANTS IN YOUR PANTS.** Be extremely restless; be unable to sit or stay still. Often said of children.

exercise 27
Mimi Decides
to Lose Weight

cut down on
cut out [S]
do with
feel up to
let . . . know

MIMI: I'll have to **cut out** cakes and pies. I'm getting fat.
SAM: You don't look fat.
MIMI: I'll turn sideways. Now **let** me **know** the truth.
SAM: A pound or two at the most. Maybe you could **do with** a little more exercise when you wake up?
MIMI: No. Exercise makes me hungry. Besides, I don't **feel up to** exercising at seven a.m.
SAM: You could **cut down on** your weight by eating fish. It isn't fattening.
MIMI: I hate fish! I'd rather stop eating first.
SAM: In Japan we eat fish all the time.
MIMI: Oh!

PART A   USING ALL FIVE IDIOMS, FILL IN THE BLANKS, ONE LETTER FOR EACH BLANK. MAKE EACH IDIOM AGREE IN TENSE AND PERSON WITH ITS SENTENCE.

Mimi has been worrying about her weight. The last few days she /_/_/_/ /_/_/_/ /_/_/_/_/_/_/_/ /_/_/_/ cake and candy entirely. Since Sam /_/_/_/ /_/_/_/ /_/_/_/_/ that she was getting fat, she decided to do without breakfast and to /_/_/ /_/_/_/_/ less food at lunch and dinner. Unfortunately he has been inviting her to play tennis every day. With all the exercise, she /_/_/_/_/_/ /_/_/_/ /_/_/ eating twice as much as before, instead of /_/_/_/_/_/_/ /_/_/_/_/ /_/_/ her food.

PART B   SOME WORDS BELOW ARE BOLD FACE. SUBSTITUTE THE ABOVE IDIOMS WHICH MEAN THE SAME THING. THEN COPY THE COMPLETE SENTENCE IN THE SAME TENSE AND PERSON.

1 I could **benefit from** a sandwich for lunch. _____

2 I have to **reduce** my consumption of whisky. _____
_____

3 I am **capable of** running ten miles this afternoon. _____

4 When you arrive in Chicago, **inform** me. _____

5 I became so nervous I had to **completely stop** drinking coffee. _____
_____

MY NAME _____ TEACHER'S NAME _____ DATE _____

PART C   WRITE THE APPROPRIATE IDIOM. MAKE IT AGREE IN TENSE AND PERSON WITH THE REST OF THE SENTENCE.

When Phil lost his job, he _____ completely any unnecessary expense. For example, he _____ his girlfriend _____ what had happened and told her not to expect any more gifts. Moreover, since he knew that he had less money to _____, he decided to _____ his everyday spending. To save money, he even _____ doing without his lunch.

PART D   FILL IN THE BLANKS, USING ALL FIVE IDIOMS PLUS ONE FROM EXERCISE 26.

Paul's wife had told him that she didn't like smoking and that she _____ he didn't smoke. His doctor had also _____ that he had better not smoke.

Paul agreed with them. He wanted to _____ smoking entirely and, in fact, had _____ it by fifty percent.

For several weeks Paul had been working day and night. He could have _____ a good night's sleep. As long as he slept enough, he _____ resisting cigarettes.

PART E   SUBSTITUTE THE CORRECT IDIOMS FOR THE BOLD FACE WORDS. THEN COPY THE WHOLE SENTENCE AND FINISH IT IN YOUR OWN WORDS.

1 After I had **completely stopped** eating candy, I. . . . _____

_____

2 Has your history professor **informed** you that. . . ? _____

_____

3 (Bob looks sick.) Is he **capable of**. . . ? _____

_____

4 We **reduced** our expenses in order to. . . . _____

_____

5 I could have **benefited from** some help when. . . . _____

_____

PART F   WRITE ONE PARAGRAPH ABOUT THE TIME YOU TRIED TO LOSE WEIGHT (OR STOP SMOKING). USE ALL FIVE IDIOMS.

COLORFUL IDIOMS: **BE TWO-FACED.** Be deceitful and hypocritical.

test 9

A. DIRECTIONS

a Rearrange the letters in each box to make an idiom and write it in the box.

b Find the definition below that fits each idiom and put its *number* in the circle.

c Add the numbers in the circles across (→) or down (↓). The numbers must total 34.

ROF NECO ◯ _____	EVAH MIH OD TI ◯ _____	STUJ WON ◯ _____	OG TUO ◯ _____ =34
KOOL ORF ◯ _____	DATESIN FO ◯ _____	TUJS HET MASE ◯ _____	EVAH NO ◯ _____ =34
DOWLU HARTER ◯ _____	ECON NI A WELHI ◯ _____	CTU TOU ◯ _____	TEL KOWN ◯ _____ =34
OD THIW ◯ _____	TUC WOND NO ◯ _____	LEFE PU OT ◯ _____	EVAH NI MDNI ◯ _____ =34
=34	=34	=34	=34

DEFINITIONS

1 suppress, stop
2 attend social or recreational events
3 be able to, be capable of
4 be wearing
5 in place of, rather than
6 prefer
7 reduce, lessen
8 for one time
9 search for, seek
10 make someone do something
11 use with benefit
12 occasionally
13 intend, plan
14 a moment ago
15 inform
16 nevertheless

MY NAME _____

TEACHER'S NAME _____ DATE _____

79

B FILL IN THE APPROPRIATE IDIOMS. USE EACH IDIOM ONLY ONCE, CHOOSING THE CORRECT TENSE AND PRONOUN.

once in a while / go out / for once / instead of / just now / would rather

1 *Ann:* "Hi Mark!" _____ I finished my homework ahead of time. It's the first time this year.

2 _____ studying tonight, I can go to the movies.

3 Would you like to _____?"

4 *Mark:* "Of course. _____ there's this detective movie playing downtown."

5 *Ann:* "Oh no! It would scare me. I _____ see a romantic film."

C FROM PART E OF EXERCISES 25, 26, 27 YOUR INSTRUCTOR WILL READ ALOUD FIVE INCOMPLETE SENTENCES. COPY THEM DOWN. THEN DO AS YOU HAVE DONE BEFORE WITH PART E: SUBSTITUTE THE IDIOMS FROM THE LIST BELOW AND FINISH THE SENTENCES IN YOUR OWN WORDS. USE AN IDIOM ONLY ONCE.

have someone do something / look for / just the same / have on / cut out / let . . .know / do with / cut down on / feel up to

1 _____

2 _____

3 _____

4 _____

5 _____

PROVERBS AND SAYINGS: IT IS NEVER TOO LATE TO MEND.

exercise 28
Mimi Has
a Toothache

get ready [S]
in the course of
put off [S]
so far
stop by

SAM: Mimi, what's the matter?
MIMI: It's my teeth. **In the course of** the last three days they've been aching all the time.
SAM: Why did you **put off** visiting the dentist?
MIMI: I was hoping the pain would stop. **So far** aspirin has helped me sleep. But I can't keep on taking it forever.
SAM: I'm going to call up my dentist and tell him it's an emergency. **Get ready**. I'll drive you to his office.
MIMI: And could we **stop by** my dressmaker. It won't take a minute.
SAM: I feel like a husband and I'm not even married.

PART A USING ALL FIVE IDIOMS, FILL IN THE BLANKS, ONE LETTER FOR EACH BLANK. MAKE EACH IDIOM AGREE IN TENSE AND PERSON WITH ITS SENTENCE.

Jane has been in Professor Smith's English class only two weeks, but / / / / / / / she likes him very much. Perhaps it is because he tells funny stories / / / / / / / / / / / / / / / / the hour.

Immediately after her English class, Jane / / / / / / / / / / / / to leave school and go home. Sometimes, however, she / / / / / / / / her boyfriend's house. Of course, she / / / / / / / / doing her homework until she gets back home.

PART B SOME WORDS BELOW ARE BOLD FACE. SUBSTITUTE THE ABOVE IDIOMS WHICH MEAN THE SAME THING. THEN COPY THE COMPLETE SENTENCE IN THE SAME TENSE AND PERSON.

1 **Prepare yourself**; our boss is calling on us. _____

2 Don't **delay** till tomorrow what you can do today. _____

_____

3 I meet many people **during** the day. _____

4 **Visit** my house; I have something for you. _____

5 **Until now** we've been lucky with our health. _____

PART C   WRITE THE APPROPRIATE IDIOM. MAKE IT AGREE IN TENSE AND PERSON WITH THE REST OF THE SENTENCE.

_____ repairing our car for a trip, the mechanic has had lots of difficulties. He has been working on it all day long, but _____ he hasn't figured out what's the matter.

A few minutes ago we _____ to leave on our trip. We _____ the automobile repair shop, but our mechanic told us our car still wasn't fixed and we had to _____ our trip again.

PART D   FILL IN THE BLANKS, USING ALL FIVE IDIOMS PLUS ONE FROM EXERCISE 27.

_____ five years Mildred has never been late to work. Why? Because she always _____ early. On the other hand, Bob has often been late to work. Why? Because he usually _____ getting dressed until the last minute.

_____ Bob has been lucky. When his boss _____ the office, he was always there. No wonder Mildred feels that she could _____ a little of Bob's luck.

PART E   SUBSTITUTE THE CORRECT IDIOMS FOR THE BOLD FACE WORDS. THEN COPY THE WHOLE SENTENCE AND FINISH IT IN YOUR OWN WORDS.

1 Mimi had **delayed** her visit to the dentist until. . . . _____
_____

2 **Until now** my parents have been pleased with. . . . _____
_____

3 We have **prepared ourselves** for. . . . _____

4 On my way to school I **visited**. . . . _____

5 **During** a long trip I usually. . . . _____

PART F   WRITE ONE PARAGRAPH ABOUT YOUR LAST VISIT TO THE DENTIST (OR DOCTOR). USE ALL FIVE IDIOMS.

COLORFUL IDIOM: **BY THE SKIN OF ONE'S TEETH.** By the smallest margin possible; barely.

exercise 29
Sam
Proposes

at heart
keep from [S]
make a difference
so much
take out [S]

SAM: Mimi, you've been crying!
MIMI: Oh Sam, I've lost a tooth. The dentist **took** it **out** this morning.
SAM: Does it hurt **so much**?
MIMI: No, it doesn't. But I'll have to wear false teeth like an old woman.
SAM: Poor darling!
MIMI: Will it **make a difference** to you? Will you still love me?
SAM: Nothing can **keep** me **from** loving you, Mimi.
MIMI: How can I be sure?
SAM: Because—because I want to marry you.
MIMI: **At heart** you just feel sorry for me.
SAM: Come here you beautiful woman!
MIMI: Ohhhhh. . . .

PART A   USING ALL FIVE IDIOMS, FILL IN THE BLANKS, ONE LETTER FOR EACH BLANK. MAKE EACH IDIOM AGREE IN TENSE AND PERSON WITH ITS SENTENCE.

Julie is rich. She has |_|_|_|_|_|_| money that she can never spend it all, but she seldom |_|_|_|_|_|_| any |_|_|_| of the bank except for very important reasons.

For years nothing has meant more to her than her money: it |_|_|_|_|_|_|_|_|_| |_|_|_|_|_|_|_|_|_|_| in her life. Unfortunately, she worries about it all the time and this |_|_|_|_|_|_|_|_|_|_| having a good time. |_|_|_|_|_|_|_| Julie is a simple woman; she loves only money.

PART B   SOME WORDS BELOW ARE BOLD FACE. SUBSTITUTE THE ABOVE IDIOMS WHICH MEAN THE SAME THING. THEN COPY THE COMPLETE SENTENCE IN THE SAME TENSE AND PERSON.

1 He seems nasty, but he's a kind man **essentially**. _____

_____

2 The dentist operated on my tooth and **removed** it. _____

_____

3 My work **prevents** me **from** having a good time. _____

MY NAME _____ TEACHER'S NAME _____ DATE _____

4 Has knowing Jim **caused changes** in your life? _____

_____

5 My mother worried **to such a great degree** about me that she became ill. _____

_____

PART C WRITE THE APPROPRIATE IDIOM. MAKE IT AGREE IN TENSE AND PERSON WITH THE REST OF THE SENTENCE.

Last week Mimi _____ her clothes _____ of the closet and, as usual, pressed them carefully. She felt it was important to look neat and well-dressed; it _____ to her.

Of course, Mimi liked buying clothes. Nothing gave her _____ happiness. A new sweater or dress always _____ feeling sad and made the world seem brighter. _____ she liked pretty clothes better than anything—even Sam.

PART D FILL IN THE BLANKS, USING ALL FIVE IDIOMS PLUS ONE FROM EXERCISE 28.

It's important to choose a good washing machine; a good machine _____ in how your clothes look. They will look cleaner because it has _____ all the dirt. It will save you time, too. Washing usually requires _____ time that either it _____ you _____ doing what you like or makes you _____ it _____ until the next day. _____ nobody likes washing.

PART E SUBSTITUTE THE CORRECT IDIOMS FOR THE BOLD FACE WORDS. THEN COPY THE WHOLE SENTENCE AND FINISH IT IN YOUR OWN WORDS.

1 Charles had drunk **such a large quantity of** alcohol that. . . . _____

_____

2 The doctor had **removed** my left eye because. . . . _____

_____

3 Using the new medicine has **caused changes** in . . . . _____

_____

4 Was your father **essentially** a sad man after. . . ? _____

_____

5 Being poor has **prevented** me **from**. . . . _____

_____

PART F WRITE ONE PARAGRAPH ABOUT THE DISADVANTAGES OF MARRIAGE. USE ALL FIVE IDIOMS.

COLORFUL IDIOM: **LOVE IS BLIND.** That is, a person in love is unable to see the imperfections of the one he loves.

exercise 30
Announcing the Engagement

fall in love with
get to
go (all) to pieces
more or less
take it easy

SAM: I'm calling up my parents to announce our engagement. You'll **get to** speak to them.

MIMI: In Japanese?

SAM: No, silly, in English. Remember, I told you my father teaches English in Kyoto. My mother **more or less** speaks it, too.

MIMI: Don't they speak any French?

SAM: **Take it easy**, Mimi. You'll only have to say a few words.

MIMI: But I feel so nervous! What if I **go (all) to pieces** and say something foolish?

SAM: Do you think I **fell in love with** you for your Oriental calm?

PART A   USING ALL FIVE IDIOMS, FILL IN THE BLANKS, ONE LETTER FOR EACH BLANK. MAKE EACH IDIOM AGREE IN TENSE AND PERSON WITH ITS SENTENCE.

Carmen is thirteen. She likes boys, and every time she / / / / / / / meet a handsome boy, she / / / / / / / / / / / / / / / / / / him. But when he doesn't love her, she becomes very sad. Then she / / / / / / / / / / / / / / / / and starts crying.

Carmen's parents know that such actions are / / / / / / / / / / / / normal for young girls, so they make her stay at home and / / / / / / / / / / for one or two days.

PART B   SOME WORDS BELOW ARE BOLD FACE. SUBSTITUTE THE ABOVE IDIOMS WHICH MEAN THE SAME THING. THEN COPY THE COMPLETE SENTENCE IN THE SAME TENSE AND PERSON.

1 Jack has **begun to love** a woman twice his age. _____

_____

2 I had **to some extent** given up smoking last year. _____

_____

3 During her driving test, she had **lost all self-control.** _____

_____

4 Have you **had the opportunity to** meet Bill Smith? _____

_____

5 You've done enough studying for today; now **relax.** _____

_____

MY NAME _____ TEACHER'S NAME _____ DATE_____

86

PART C   WRITE THE APPROPRIATE IDIOM. MAKE IT AGREE IN TENSE AND PERSON WITH THE REST OF THE SENTENCE.

Tom was very emotional. Every time he _____ kiss a pretty girl, he _____ her. As a result, he was _____ in love all the time.

However, when his girlfriends didn't love him, he _____ and didn't sleep nights. He couldn't relax and _____ any more.

PART D   FILL IN THE BLANKS, USING ALL FIVE IDIOMS PLUS ONE FROM EXERCISE 29.

Mimi _____ know Sam while they were studying English together. At first, they went out as many as four times a week. Later, however, they sometimes did nothing. They just _____ . Mimi soon _____ Sam. Of course, we _____ expected this. But we didn't think she would _____ when she spoke to Sam's parents. It seems that the experience shocked her _____ that Sam had to do all the talking.

PART E   SUBSTITUTE THE CORRECT IDIOMS FOR THE BOLD FACE WORDS. THEN COPY THE WHOLE SENTENCE AND FINISH IT IN YOUR OWN WORDS.

1 Caroline usually **relaxed** while she. . . . _____
2 Sam had **had the opportunity to**. . .at Mimi's party. _____
_____
3 Mr. Green had **lost all self-control** when. . . . _____
_____
4 I was **to some extent** tired after. . . . _____
5 Sam had **begun to love** Mimi because. . . . _____
_____

PART F   WRITE ONE PARAGRAPH ABOUT THE ADVANTAGES OF MARRIAGE. USE ALL FIVE IDIOMS.

COLORFUL IDIOM: **PUPPY LOVE:** Immature or youthful affection; the kind of love that teenagers usually experience.

test 10

A. DIRECTIONS

a   Rearrange the letters in each box to make an idiom and write it in the box.

b   Find the definition below that fits each idiom and put its *number* in the circle.

c   Add the numbers in the circles across (———►) or down (▼). The numbers must total 34.

DEFINITIONS

1   during
2   cause changes
3   relax
4   have the opportunity to
5   somewhat, to some extent
6   until now
7   omit, forego
8   remove, extract
9   essentially
10   a very large quantity; to a very great degree
11   lose all self-control
12   postpone, delay
13   become very fond of someone
14   visit
15   prepare yourself
16   refrain from

NI HTE ERSCUO FO	OS FRA	TGE DEARY	TUP FOF
◯ ___	◯ ___	◯ ___	◯ ___ =34
POTS Y B	KATE TOU	KEAM A EIDERNFECF	OS CUMH
◯ ___	◯ ___	◯ ___	◯ ___ =34
EPEK MORF	TA THARE	TEG OT	ROME RO SELS
◯ ___	◯ ___	◯ ___	◯ ___ =34
KAET TI YASE	OG OT SPICEE	LAFL NI VOLE THIW	OD TUTHOWI
◯ ___	◯ ___	◯ ___	◯ ___
=34	=34	=34	=34

87

B   FILL IN THE APPROPRIATE IDIOMS. USE EACH IDIOM ONLY ONCE, CHOOSING THE CORRECT TENSE AND PRONOUN.

stop by / so much / fall in love with / more or less / get ready / put off

1 Mary _____ Frank the first time she saw him.

2 When she has a date with Frank, she _____ an hour ahead of time.

3 In fact, she _____ everything else to the next day.

4 When he _____ unexpectedly, she becomes very excited.

5 She loves him _____ that she would like to marry him.

C   FROM PART E OF EXERCISES 28, 29, 30 YOUR INSTRUCTOR WILL READ ALOUD FIVE INCOMPLETE SENTENCES. COPY THEM DOWN. THEN DO AS YOU HAVE DONE BEFORE WITH PART E: SUBSTITUTE THE IDIOMS FROM THE LIST BELOW AND FINISH THE SENTENCES IN YOUR OWN WORDS. USE AN IDIOM ONLY ONCE.

in the course of / so far / take out / make a difference / keep from / at heart / get to / take it easy / go (all) to pieces

1 _____

2 _____

3 _____

4 _____

5 _____

PROVERBS AND SAYINGS: IT'S THE LAST STRAW THAT BREAKS THE CAMEL'S BACK.

Alphabetical Idiom List

A

20* about to
SE ahead of time
22 all along
12 all day long
18 all of a sudden
11 all right
13 all the time
13 as far as
10 as for
20 ask for [S]**
21 as long as
4 as many as
2 as much as
15 as usual
7 as well as
21 as yet
11 at all
SE at first
29 at heart
3 at home
15 at least
7 at (the) most

B

19 be a question of
5 be used to
9 bring up [S]
16 by far
17 by the way

C

23 call off [S]
12 call on
22 call up [S]
8 catch cold
2 change (one's) mind
2 come from
27 cut down on
27 cut out [S]

D

SE do one's best
27 do with
11 do without

E

21 even so
24 every other

F

30 fall in love with
27 feel up to
16 figure out [S]
8 find fault with
9 find out [S]
25 for once
12 for the time being
1 from now on

G

13 get back
SE get mixed up
3 get off
3 get on
28 get ready [S]
2 get rid of
30 get to
24 give back [S]
9 give up [S]
22 go away
2 go on
25 go out (to)
11 go too far
30 go (all) to pieces
18 go up

H

6 had better
7 have a good time
25 have (someone) do (something)
23 have in mind [S]
26 have on [S]
11 have over [S]
3 have to
9 How's that?

I

10 in a hurry
5 in fact
26 instead of
28 in the course of
13 in the first place
4 in the long run
6 in time
19 it's a question of
7 (it's) no wonder

J

25 just now
26 just the same

K

29 keep from [S]
16 keep on + ing
23 keep quiet [S]
14 keep up with

L

16 leave out [S]
19 let (somebody) alone
27 let (somebody) know
17 let (me, us) see
24 let go of
1 little by little

H (cont.)

17 look at
25 look for
15 look forward to + ing
16 look into
23 look up [S]

M

29 make a difference
12 make a living
14 make a point of
22 make fun of
24 make out [S]
10 make sense
15 make sure
15 make the most of
20 might as well
18 more and more
30 more or less

N

19 no matter
19 not much of a
7 (it's) no wonder

O

SE of course
21 once and for all
26 once in a while
22 on purpose
9 on the other hand
5 on the whole
6 on time
20 outside of

P

10 put in [S]
28 put off [S]

*Numbers 1-30 = Exercises 1-30.   SE = Sample Exercise
**[S] after an idiom means that an American or English speaker often *separates* it by inserting a noun or a pronoun between its words.
EXAMPLE: ASK FOR [S]   She *asked for* a drink.
She *asked* Bill *for* a drink.
She *asked* him *for* a drink.

8 put on [S]
14 put up with

Q

6 quite a few

R

23 read up on
5 right away
3 run into
24 run out of

S

4 see about
28 so far

29 so much
12 sooner or later
21 step by step
28 stop by

T

7 take advantage of
4 take a trip
1 take care of
30 take it easy
29 take out [S]
17 take part in
20 take place
4 take turns
18 take up [S]
6 talk (something) over [S]
19 tell A from B

1 that's all
17 that is
5 think of
8 think (something) over [S]
8 time after time
14 turn off [S]
14 turn on [S]

U

18 up to
13 used to

W

10 What about. . .?
1 What's the matter?
26 would rather

CONTRACTIONS USED IN THIS BOOK

isn't	is not	*I'm*	I am	*you'd*	you had; you would
aren't	are not	*you're*	you are	*he'd*	he had; he would
wasn't	was not	*he's*	he is, he has	*she'd*	she had; she would
weren't	were not	*she's*	she is, she has	*it'd*	it had; it would
haven't	have not	*it's*	it is, it has	*we'd*	we had; we would
hasn't	has not	*we're*	we are	*they'd*	they had; they would
hadn't	had not	*they're*	they are	*who's*	who is
don't	do not	*I'll*	I will	*what's*	what is
doesn't	does not	*you'll*	you will	*when's*	when is
didn't	did not	*he'll*	he will	*where's*	where is
won't	will not	*she'll*	she will	*how's*	how is
wouldn't	would not	*it'll*	it will	*that's*	that is
shan't	shall not	*we'll*	we will	*there's*	there is
shouldn't	should not	*they'll*	they will	*here's*	here is
can't	can not	*I've*	I have		
couldn't	could not	*you've*	you have		
mightn't	might not	*we've*	we have		
oughtn't	ought not	*they've*	they have		
mustn't	must not	*I'd*	I had; I would		

Index

*Although the same idiom may have different meanings (*a, b, c,* etc.), it will have only meaning (*a*) in the Exercise.

*[S]   indicates a separable idiom. A noun or pronoun may be inserted between its words.
  Example: ASK FOR [S]   She **asked** Bill **for** a drink.
                        She **asked** him **for** a drink.

AT FIRST   page 3   at the beginning

At first, I hated American food. However, I soon learned to like it.

AT HEART   page 83   essentially, fundamentally

Jack can be impolite, but at heart he's a good fellow.

AT HOME   page 11   in one's house

Phone me tonight. I'll be at home.

AT LEAST   page 43   not less than

They need at least three hours to finish their work.

AT (THE) MOST   page 23   not more than, maximum

We can give you five dollars at the most. Don't ask for more.

B

BE A QUESTION OF   page 57   see IT'S A QUESTION OF

BE USED TO   page 17   be accustomed to

Eskimos are used to snow and ice.

BRING UP [S]   page 27   a   raise (a subject or question), introduce a subject into a discussion

Mary's father died last week. Don't bring up his name when you meet her.

b   care for in childhood, rear

My mother brought up seven children.

BY FAR   page 49   greatly, obviously, by a great margin

Mary is by far the prettiest girl in our class.

BY THE WAY   page 51   incidentally, in that connection (but of secondary interest)

I don't intend to invite Bill to my party. By the way, he won't be surprised. He knows I don't like him.

C

CALL OFF [S]   page 67   cancel; decide against doing, having, etc.

It was raining, so our coach called off the baseball game.

CALL ON   page 35   a   visit

Every time I go to Philadelphia, I call on my sister.

b   ask to participate or contribute

My professor is always calling on me in class.

CALL UP [S]   page 65   a   telephone

I'll call you up tomorrow at nine.

b   bring to mind

The old film called up my boyhood memories.

CATCH COLD   page 25   become ill with a cold

When I drive my car with its windows open, I catch cold.

CHANGE (ONE'S) MIND   page 9   alter one's decision

We changed our mind. We're not going to Europe next summer.

COME FROM   page 9   a   be a native of

My classmates come from twelve different countries.

b   derive from, originate in

Many English words come from Latin.

CUT DOWN ON   page 77   reduce, lessen

You must cut down on your expenses if you want to save money.

CUT OUT [S]   page 77   a   suppress, stop
The best way to lose weight is to **cut out** eating candy.
                              b   remove by cutting around; excise
The boy **cut out** pictures from the magazine.

D

DO (ONE'S) BEST   page 3   try hard to do something well
I **do my best** to get good marks in English.
DO WITH   page 77   a   profit from, use with advantage
I'm cold. I could **do with** a hot cup of coffee.
                    b   manage with (for lack of something better)
Since Alice doesn't own an overcoat, she must **do with** a sweater in winter.
DO WITHOUT   page 33   manage without, live without something
In the United States, people cannot **do without** a car. Distances are too great.

E

EVEN SO   page 61   however, regardless, nevertheless
Al buys his wife everything she wants. **Even so**, she isn't happy.
EVERY OTHER   page 69   every second one, alternate
In summer I take a bath every day, but in winter **every other** day is enough.

F

FALL IN LOVE WITH   page 85   begin to love someone; feel a strong, usually passionate, affection for
John **falls in love with** every pretty girl he meets.
FEEL UP TO   page 77   be able to, feel capable of
I slept so well that I **feel up to** playing tennis before breakfast.
FIGURE OUT [S]   page 49   a   understand; discover by reason
I can't **figure out** why Bob quit his job. I thought he liked it.
                    b   calculate, solve
Do you **figure out** your income tax every year?
FIND FAULT WITH   page 25   criticize, complain about, be dissatisfied with
My boss doesn't like me, so he always tries to **find fault with** my work.
FIND OUT [S]   page 27   learn, discover
How did you **find out** that he wasn't telling the truth?
FOR ONCE   page 73   this one time
For once, I was able to do what I always wanted: I spent the whole month swimming.
FOR THE TIME BEING   page 35   temporarily, for the present moment
You can live with us **for the time being**, but you must find your own apartment soon.
FROM NOW ON   page 7   starting now and continuing into the future; from this time forward
For months our class started at 8:00 a.m. **From now on** it will start at 9:00 a.m.

G

GET BACK   page 39   return
When did you **get back** from London? (same meaning: COME BACK)
GET MIXED UP   page 3   become confused
Carol **got mixed up** in the dates. She thought that March 21st was your birthday.

GET OFF   page 11   a   descend from, leave (a bus, train, plane, boat)
We **got off** the bus at Fifth Avenue.
                     b   remove from [S]
The ring was too tight. Doris couldn't **get it off** her finger.
GET ON   page 11   a   go into, enter (a bus, train, plane, boat)
Jill **got on** the plane and flew to Chicago.
                     b   live or work in friendship with someone
Jim and his brother never fight. They **get on** well together.
GET READY [S]   page 81   a   prepare yourself
Can you **get ready** to leave by 6:00 p.m.?
                     b   prepare something [S]
Could you **get** the dinner **ready** early tonight?
GET RID OF   page 9   discard, eliminate, throw away
If I had more money, I would **get rid of** my old car and buy a new one.
GET TO   page 85   a   succeed in
Freddy finally **got to** enter college and his mother was pleased.
                     b   arrive
The train **gets to** New York at noon.
GIVE BACK [S]   page 24   return
Give me **back** my book. I need it for my homework.
GIVE UP [S]   page 27   a   abandon, stop, renounce
Smoking is bad for your health. You ought to **give it up**.
                     b   surrender
When the robbers realized they couldn't escape, they **gave up**.
GO AWAY   page 65   depart, leave
My brother **goes away** to school this fall.
GO ON   page 9   a   happen
I wonder what **is going on** in the United States. I haven't read our newspaper for a week.
                     b   continue
It's early. We can **go on** playing football for another hour.
GO OUT (TO)   page 73   a   attend social or recreational activities
We try not to **go out** more than twice a week. We're too tired afterwards.
                     b   leave
Janet **went out** a few minutes ago.
                     c   stop burning, stop producing heat or light
Add some more wood to the fire or it will **go out**.
GO TOO FAR   page 33   pass beyond a certain limit
Bill **goes too far** when he lies to his own mother.
GO (ALL) TO PIECES   page 85   lose all self-control
After her husband's death, Olga **went (all) to pieces** and cried for a whole month.
GO UP   page 53   a   rise, increase
Food prices have been **going up** for two years now.
                     b   ascend, mount
If you **go up** those stairs, be careful. The third step is broken.

H

HAD BETTER   page 19   ought to, would be wise to
If you want to pass that exam, you **had better** study.

HAVE A GOOD TIME   page 23   enjoy oneself

I **had a good time** at your party. I danced the whole evening.

HAVE (SOMEONE) DO (SOMETHING)   page 73   make somebody do something, cause him to do it

My mother **has me finish my homework** before I watch TV.

HAVE IN MIND   page 67   intend, plan

I **had in mind** going to a play tonight. O.K.?

HAVE ON [S]   page 75   a   be wearing

Did Beth **have** her green dress **on** last night?

HAVE OVER [S]   page 33   invite

We would like to **have you over** for dinner next week. (In British usage: **have in.**)

HAVE TO   page 11   must, ought to

Every day I **have to** be at the office at nine sharp.

HOW'S THAT?   page 27   How is it possible? Explain what you mean.

You say John is sick! **How's that?** I just met him in the street.

I

IN A HURRY   page 31   rushed, with a need to move or act quickly

Bill's **in a hurry**. His plane leaves in ten minutes.

IN FACT   page 17   really, indeed, in reality

George is very religious. **In fact**, he wants to become a priest.

INSTEAD OF   page 75   in place of, rather than

When I went in his room, my brother was sleeping **instead of** studying.

IN THE COURSE OF   page 81   during

In the course of his life, Henry worked hard.

IN THE FIRST PLACE   page 39   firstly, to begin with

I can't go with you tonight. **In the first place**, I feel sick. In the second place, I have an exam tomorrow.

IN THE LONG RUN   page 15   with time, eventually, finally

When I first met Jim, I didn't like him. But **in the long run** he proved to be a good friend.

IN TIME   page 19   early enough

I rarely come home **in time** to watch the six o'clock news on TV.

IT'S A QUESTION OF   page 57   it concerns

We cannot go to Europe this summer. **It's not a question of** money; **it's a question of** time.

IT'S NO WONDER   page 23   see NO WONDER

J

JUST NOW   page 73   a minute ago, this very moment

You can still catch Jane on the stairs. She left **just now**.

JUST THE SAME   page 75   a   nevertheless

I told her not to leave, but she left **just the same**.

                                        b   in the same way

Mary is 40 years old now, but she dresses **just the same** as when she was 20.

K

KEEP FROM [S]   page 83   restrain or refrain from; prevent

Bill looked so funny that I couldn't **keep from** laughing.

As it fell, I grabbed the glass and **kept** it **from** breaking.

KEEP ON + ING   page 49   continue
    Dan is stupid. He **keeps on** making the same mistakes.
    The rain **kept on** falling for seven days.

KEEP QUIET [S]   page 67   a   remain silent
    Keep quiet and listen to me.
                              b   stop (someone or something) from making noise
    Keep him **quiet** while I'm studying.

KEEP UP WITH   page 41   a   be aware of
    I try to **keep up with** what's happening in the world.
                              b   go or move as fast as
    Mike walks so fast his wife can't **keep up with** him.

L

LEAVE OUT [S]   page 49   omit
    When Mary told the story, she **left out** some important facts.

LET (SOMEBODY) ALONE   page 57   allow somebody to be undisturbed
    Let me alone. I have to study for my test.

LET (SOMEBODY) KNOW   page 77   inform, tell
    Let me know when you are ready and we shall go.

LET (ME, US) SEE   page 51   allow me to think, to consider
    (Hello! I would like to make an appointment with the dentist.)
    Well, **let me see.** Can you come tomorrow at 2:00 p.m.?

LET GO OF   page 69   release
    Don't **let go of** the bottle or it will fall.

LITTLE BY LITTLE   page 7   gradually
    I'm losing a pound a week. **Little by little** I'm becoming thin.

LOOK AT   page 51   a   direct one's eyes toward, direct one's attention toward
    Look at your dog! He's eating the roast!
                              b   consider, examine
    Look at the life he lives. It's horrible!

LOOK FOR [S]   page 73   search for, seek
    Would you help me **look for** my keys? I think I've lost them.

LOOK FORWARD TO + ING   page 43   anticipate with pleasure
    I'm looking forward to going to Japan.
    I look forward to your visit next month.

LOOK INTO   page 49   investigate, examine
    The police **looked into** the robbery.

LOOK UP [S]   page 67   a   research, search in a book
    Wait a minute! Let me **look up** the exact address in the phonebook.
    I **looked** it **up** for you.
                              b   improve, prosper
    Business is **looking up** again. I sold three cars last week.

M

MAKE A DIFFERENCE   page 83   a   change the situation, cause a change
    The death of my father **made a** big **difference** in our life.
                              b   matter, be of importance
    It doesn't **make a difference** to me whether you come tonight or not.

MAKE A LIVING   page 35   earn enough to live adequately
   He works days and nights to **make a living**.
MAKE A POINT OF   page 41   insist upon, give importance to
   My mother **makes a point of** remembering my birthday.
MAKE FUN OF   page 65   laugh at, ridicule
   When Hélène speaks English, her friends **make fun of** her accent.
MAKE OUT [S]   page 69   a   understand, interpret
   Can you **make out** why she behaves so rudely?
                           b   identify, distinguish
   It's too dark. I can't **make out** the street numbers.
MAKE SENSE   page 31   be intelligible, be reasonable
   Henry tells us that he is poor. It doesn't **make sense** because I know he earns $15,000 a year.
MAKE SURE   page 43   be certain, cause to be certain
   I **made sure** the door was locked before I left.
MAKE THE MOST OF   page 43   use to the greatest advantage
   I **make the most of** my vacations: I ski in the morning, play bridge in the afternoon, and dance at night.
MIGHT AS WELL   page 59   could do with equal or better effect, is somewhat preferable
   I have finished my work. I **might as well** go home now.
   Since your car is broken, you **might as well** sleep here tonight.
MORE AND MORE   page 53   increasingly
   John works too hard. He is becoming **more and more** tired.
MORE OR LESS   page 85   somewhat, to some extent
   Bob drinks too much. He is **more or less** drunk every time I see him.

N

NO MATTER   page 57   regardless of
   No matter how well I do my work, my boss always finds something wrong.
NOT MUCH OF A   page 57   rather bad
   A noisy motel is **not much of a** place to sleep.
NO WONDER   page 23   naturally, it is not surprising
   (It's) no wonder he didn't arrive! His airplane crashed.

O

OF COURSE   page 3   naturally
   Are you coming to our party? **Of course**, I am. I love parties.
ONCE AND FOR ALL   page 61   finally, permanently, conclusively
   Once and for all do what I tell you! I won't say it again.
ONCE IN A WHILE   page 75   occasionally
   Our son comes to see us **once in a while**, mainly when he needs money.
ON PURPOSE   page 65   intentionally, for a reason
   She broke that glass **on purpose**. She was really angry.
ON THE OTHER HAND   page 27   from the opposite point of view
   I like winters in Florida; **on the other hand**, I prefer the cool summers of Maine.
ON THE WHOLE   page 17   a   in general
   On the whole, Americans are nice people.
                           b   all things considered
   Sam doesn't always attend class, but **on the whole** he is a good student.

ON TIME   page 19   punctually, exactly at a fixed time
    Our train is rarely **on time**; it can be as much as 15 minutes late.
OUTSIDE OF   page 59   other than, except for
    Outside of golf, I don't like sports.

P

PUT IN [S]   page 31   a   to spend time in a specified manner
    It's a shame Jeff failed his exam. He **put in** a whole week studying for it.
                              b   insert
    If you write to Jane, **put in** a few words about my trip.
PUT OFF [S]   page 81   a   postpone, delay
    You complain about your health, but you always **put off** going to the doctor.
                                b   evade answering questions or giving information
    Each time I ask for my money back, Jack **puts** me **off**.
PUT ON [S]   page 25   a   dress in, clothe oneself
    Shall I **put on** a long dress for the party?
                                  b   add
    Last year Matthew **put on** ten pounds. Now he looks fat.
PUT UP WITH   page 41   tolerate
    Fred **put up with** his wife's bad temper for years, but finally he divorced her.

Q

QUITE A FEW   page 19   more than a few, a lot of
    This restaurant must be good; there are **quite a few** people in it.

R

READ UP ON   page 67   study by reading about
    I'm reading up on American history because I have an exam in it tomorrow.
RIGHT AWAY   page 17   immediately
    Please wait a minute. Anita said that she would come back **right away**.
RUN INTO   page 11   a   meet by chance
    Yesterday, I **ran into** an old friend on the street. What a pleasant surprise to see him again!
                                b   crash into, collide with
    He **ran into** me with his car and broke my legs.
RUN OUT OF   page 69   come to the end of, exhaust a supply of something
    My car **ran out of** gas on the highway.

S

SEE ABOUT   page 15   attend to, take charge of, occupy yourself with
    Wait in the car! I'll **see about** finding a hotel for tonight.
SO FAR   page 81   until now
    So far we are quite satisfied with the car we bought last month.
SO FAR AS   see AS FAR AS
SO LONG AS   see AS LONG AS

SO MUCH   page 83   a   adj. considerable, a very large quantity of

I have **so much** work that I won't be able to finish before supper.

b   adv. considerably, to such a great degree

I studied **so much** that I'm very tired.

SOONER OR LATER   page 35   inevitably, ultimately, eventually

You'll have to study **sooner or later**. Why not now?

STEP BY STEP   page 61   gradually, by degrees

Step by step the boy learned to read.

STOP BY   page 81   visit, pass by

On our way home, we **stopped by** Jim's house for a few minutes.

We'll **stop by** at seven o'clock and take you to the play.

T

TAKE ADVANTAGE OF   page 23   a   profit from, make use of

We **took advantage of** our trip to Japan to buy a new camera.

b   gain at the expense of another; use unfairly

The salesman **took advantage of** my ignorance to sell me a bad TV set.

TAKE A TRIP   page 15   go for a journey

Every summer I **take a trip** to Europe.

TAKE CARE OF   page 7   a   give attention to

I must **take care of** my sore throat or it will get worse.

b   use or treat with care

Take care of your shoes and they'll last a long time.

c   look after, be responsible for

My sister **takes care of** my children while I go shopping.

TAKE IT EASY   page 85   relax

Take it easy! The dentist said it wouldn't hurt you.

I've been working for several weekends. This weekend I'm going to **take it easy**.

TAKE OUT [S]   page 83   a   remove, extract

He **took out** his wallet and gave me the money.

b   accompany, escort

Sorry, I cannot go with you tonight. Henry **takes** me **out** every Saturday.

TAKE PART IN   page 51   participate

Today, I **took part in** a class discussion on abortion.

TAKE PLACE   page 59   happen, occur

We told Fanny what **took place** in her absence. She was shocked.

TAKE TURNS   page 15   alternate

When we travel by car, my wife and I **take turns** driving.

TAKE UP [S]   page 53   a   undertake, begin, adopt

On his doctor's recommendation, Harry **took up** golf as an exercise.

b   occupy space or time

That bed **takes up** too much space in my room.

TALK (SOMETHING) OVER page 19   discuss

Fanny and Sam **talked over** their vacation plans.

TELL A FROM B   page 57   distinguish between

Barbara and Betty are twins. When I meet them, I can never **tell Barbara from Betty**.

THAT'S ALL   page 7   only that, nothing more

Aren't you eating anything else for lunch? No, **that's all!** I want to lose weight.

THAT IS   page 51   to say it more exactly

I wish I could speak English, **that is**, speak it well.

THINK OF   page 17   a   have an opinion

What do you **think of** my new dress?

b   consider, intend to

We **are thinking of** buying a new house.

THINK (SOMETHING) OVER [S]   page 25   consider carefully before deciding

Don't decide now. **Think** it **over** for a few days, and then give me your answer.

TIME AFTER TIME   page 25   repeatedly

Time after time our teacher told us to study hard.

TURN OFF [S]   page 41   shut off, close, stop

Don't leave the water running. **Turn** it **off**, please.

Please **turn off** the lights before you leave the room.

TURN ON [S]   page 41   let come, let flow, open

It's getting dark. **Turn** the lights **on**, please.

U

UP TO   page 53   until

Up to now I did well in English, but today I failed my test.

USED TO   page 39   had the habit of, formerly did

I **used to** smoke three packages of cigarettes a day.

W

WHAT ABOUT . . . ?   page 31   a   How would you like. . . ?

It has been a hot day. **What about** a cool drink?

b   request for information

My mother has recovered from her accident. **What about** your father?

WHAT'S THE MATTER?   page 7   What's happening? What's wrong?

What's the matter? You look very pale suddenly!

WOULD RATHER   page 75   prefer

I'd rather see a movie than study tonight.

I **would rather** live than die.

1. **Error:**   *As usual,* John gets up at six a.m.
    Correction: a) John gets up at six a.m. (idiom deleted)
                       b) *As usual*, John is getting up at six a.m.
    Comment: *As usual* is probably an elliptical clause of comparison: *as he usually* does. If so, you cannot say: *AS he USUALly gets up at six a.m., John gets up at six a.m.* No comparison is possible inasmuch as both the subordinate clause and the main clause express the *identical* notion of customary action. On the other hand, correction *b* works because you can compare the notion of customary action (as expressed by *as usual*) with a future act (*is getting up at six a.m.*).

2. **Error:**   I will *get back* to my country soon.
    Correction: I will go back to my country soon.
    Comment: *Get back* means *come back*. My students—I suspect—were thinking of returning to their own countries. [They may also have been thinking of their country as *here*, forgetting that they were presently somewhere else (the U.S.), which had now, geographically, become *here* for them.]

3. **Error:**   You don't *have to* leave now. You must stay.
    Correction: a) You mustn't leave now. You must stay.
                       b) You don't *have to* leave now. Can't you stay?
    Comment: The above pair of "erroneous" sentences (with the right intonation) could be correct for natives but would probably indicate for my ESL students that *don't have to* meant *must not*. They ought to have known that the negative of this idiom recommends, not commands.

4. **Error:**   I came to class *in time*.
    Correction: a) I came to class *on time*.
                       b) I came *in time* to ask my teacher a question before class began.
    Comment: *On time* means a particular time—a *point* of time. You must either arrive at that time or you'll arrive late. By way of contrast, *in time*, means a sufficient *amount* of time to do or experience something.

5. **Error:**   I tried to *keep from* small towns all my life.
    Correction: a) I tried to *keep away from* small towns all my life.
                       b) I tried all my life to *keep from* living in small towns.
    Comment: Both *keep from* and *keep away from* mean *avoid*, but the former idiom precedes V + ING whereas the latter idiom precedes N.

6. **Error:**   *Outside of* the U.S., I like only Mexico.
    Correction: Except for the U.S., I like only Mexico.
    Comment: An unintentional pun: *outside of* means both *location* and *exception*.

7. **Error:**   *So far* she became a good teacher.
    Correction: *So far* she has been a good teacher.
    Comment: This idiom conveys the notion of the past continuing into the present; therefore, use a present perfect verb.

8. **Error:**   I like *so much* the United States.
    Correction: a) I like the United States *so much* that I am going to stay here.
                       b) I like the United States very much.
    Comment: *So much* should be followed here by an adverbial that-clause. In this instance, the student probably confused *so much* with *very much*.

9. **Error:**   My bus *took* me *out* for a good time.
    Correction: My girlfriend *took* me *out* for a good time.
    Comment: This idiom involves a semantic constraint: It is +human, -animal, -inanimate.

10. **Error:**   I *used to* work hard, but today I am taking it easy.
    Correction: a) I *used to* work hard, but now I take it easy.
                       b) I *am used to* working hard, but today (exceptionally) I am taking it easy.
    Comment: *Used to* conveys the notion of past repetition which has recently changed its frequency or stopped. However, if it is only "today" during which "I am taking it easy," this suggests that "I" continue to work hard in the present. Therefore, the first clause of the sentence contradicts the second.

A STUDENT'S LOG[1] OF IDIOMATIC ENGLISH

(Occasions on which you or somebody else USED[2] an IDIOM[3] outside class)

TO THE TEACHER: This LOG is intended to promote class discussion of English usage and to help students define their language problems more exactly.

Name: _____

Dates: _____ to _____

Idiom Used	How the Idiom was Used[4]	Persons Involved	Purpose (or reason)	Topic (or event)	Place	What were the circumstances? Why did using the idiom seem to succeed or fail?	Day and Time
Example: take it easy	face-to-face	A teacher and me.	To apologize by saying something kind.	My bumping into another person.	In the hall outside my English class.	I said, "Take it easy," because the teacher seemed upset and I wanted him to relax. He replied that I was impolite. Perhaps I can't use this idiom with some people.	April 3 2 p.m.

1. Log = record
2. Used = spoken, heard, read, or written.
3. Idiom = any idiom, in your book or not.

4. **How used** = face-to-face, overheard, on the phone, in writing, on TV, on radio, in a magazine, etc.